JOSEPH OF ARIMATHEA

THE MAN WHO BURIED JESUS

Joseph of Arimathea

The Man Who Buried Jesus

A HISTORICAL NOVEL BY

Robert Cruikshank

Order this book online at www.trafford.com
or email orders@trafford.com

Most Trafford titles are also available at major online book retailers.

Printed in the United States of America.

ISBN: 978-1-4269-5833-5 (sc)
ISBN: 978-1-4269-5834-2 (e)

Trafford rev. 02/11/2011

 www.trafford.com

North America & international
toll-free: 1 888 232 4444 (USA & Canada)
phone: 250 383 6864 ♦ fax: 812 355 4082

Dedication

It is with endearing reverence that I dedicate this book
in loving memory of my sweet mother,
Thelma Evelyn Hopkins Cruikshank,
16 August 1912—17 October 1979
whose love nurtured my formative years,
whose wisdom inspired my childhood days,
and
whose often told stories about her ancestors
and the Scarlet Thread
still excite me.

Forward

This historical novel brings together modern research and ancient legends which trace the journey of Joseph of Arimathea from England on his annual pilgrimage to Palestine where, during this particular trip, his world is turned upside down by the political crucifixion of Jesus at the hands of those old enemies who envy and despise the royal members of David's line. Joseph of Arimathea, with Nicodemus, buries Jesus' body according to Jewish ritual. For this, Joseph is himself arrested, but he is delivered from imprisonment by the risen Jesus. As an ardent believer in and a follower of God's chosen One, Joseph plays a vital role in establishing the Early Church and its subsequent missionary movement. After fourteen years in Palestine, Joseph returns to England as a missionary. He is sent there as the first bishop to England and Wales, and builds a church at Glastonbury. Joseph carries with him to England the silver chalice and silver plate used during the Last Supper, along with a staff fashioned from the crown of thorns placed on Jesus' head. The silver chalice contained a substantial amount of blood saved from the burial of Jesus. The staff of thorns was stuck into the ground at Glastonbury and miraculously took root. It remains today as "The Holy Thorn of Glastonbury." The silver chalice and plate remained at Glastonbury until they were returned to Jerusalem by Helena, a descendant of Joseph and, herself, a passionate believer in Christ. Some would later refer to the chalice as "The Holy Grail." Helena's son, also an ardent follower of Christ, would become Constantine the Great, Emperor of Rome. It was he who ended the systematic persecution of Christians. An appendix depicts some of the surviving descendant lines of the two children of Joseph of Arimathea and his wife Anna.

Table of Contents

Chapter 1 – Going Home
   Joseph Returns to Palestine from England   1

Chapter 2 – News from Home
   Ponders the events taking place in Palestine   4

Chapter 3 – Signs of Promise
   Business and religious duties   8

Chapter 4 – In Pursuit of Truth
   Visits family and seeks the truth about Jesus   15

Chapter 5 – Joy in Believing
   Visits Jesus and learns He is the anointed of God 22

Chapter 6 – O Jerusalem
   Jesus goes to Jerusalem   30

Chapter 7 – A Time of Choices
   People decide who Jesus is   38

Chapter 8 – The Night of Horrors
   Jesus is arrested, Joseph tries to intervene   45

Chapter 9 – A Time of Reflection
   Joseph reflects on Jesus' boyhood   52

Chapter 10 – Thoughts of Yesterday
   Joseph recalls Jesus' visit to Cornwall   56

Chapter 11 – Day of the Cross
   Joseph watches Jesus being crucified   61

Chapter 12 – Deed of Honor
   Joseph buries Jesus according to Jewish custom   67

Chapter 13 – Imprisonment
   Joseph is accosted by an angry Council and Jailed 70

Chapter 14 – Miraculous Delivery
    Joseph is delivered from his prison cell by Jesus   73

Chapter 15 – Attempted Reconciliation
    The Council apologizes and Joseph attempts reconciliation   78

Chapter 16 – A Different Path Taken
    Joseph and the Council take different paths   83

Chapter 17 – A Higher Calling
    Council persecutes Church, Joseph lends assistance   89

Chapter 18 – The Broader Vision
    Joseph returns to England - The Glastonbury mission   97

Chapter 19 – Followers of The Way
    Joseph of Arimathea's legacy   102

Chapter 20 – Epilogue
    Searching for truth among facts and legends   111

Appendix
    Some Descendants of Joseph of Arimathea and Anna   117

Chapter 1 – Going Home

He was up at dawn. By the time Joseph of Arimathea had finished packing his belongings, however, the sun was high in the morning sky as he made his way to the ship's forward deck.

It had been twenty-four days since his journey to Jerusalem began and, now, from his position near the bow of the ship, Joseph could vaguely detect the outline of the Palestinian hills. The sight of those sacred summits sent an anxious tingle racing throughout his entire body.

He was rewarded by the scent of a familiar smell coming from those hills. Its sweet aroma wafted on the easterly breeze now blowing in his face, as if reaching out to welcome him home. His visit to Palestine this year was different from those journeys he had made in the past but, as yet, Joseph held no inkling of how monumentally different this particular visit home to Palestine and Jerusalem would turn out to be.

His journey had started in Siluria (which would later be called Monmouth shire), in England. He sailed in a small boat down the river Gwy, to Offa, on the river Severn. He had been accompanied on the trip to Offa by Bran and Amalech, his son and grandson. Amalech was a bright-eyed lad of ten years. He had always delighted in hearing the many stories told to him by his grandparents about his ancestors.

The following day Joseph boarded a different vessel and, from the deck of the ship, waved farewell to Bran and Amalech. The ship on which he took passage would soon sail into the Bristol Channel and around the horn of Cornwall to the port of Burdigala (Bordeaux), in France. Burdigala (Bordeux) was situated on the Gulf of Biscay.

He arrived in Buordigala (Bordeaux) after seven days at sea. The weather thus far had been pleasantly accommodating, considering it was the third week in March (the month of Adar for those who use the Jewish calendar).

The ship on which he took passage encountered only one small squall during its entire journey from Offa to Burdigala (Bordeaux), that being the day before they reached the port there. On other occasions, when members of his family had accompanied him on these journeys to Palestine, they had made the entire voyage by ship, sailing from Burdigala (Bordeaux) around Spain to the port of Cadiz, thence through the Straits of Gibraltar and into the Mediterranean Sea.

That longer sea trip could take Joseph and his family as long as forty days or more. This time, however, Joseph of Arimathea had delayed in leaving, he traveled alone, and he was in a hurry to reach Palestine.

After one day of rest in Burdigala (Bordeaux), another six days took him overland through the province of modern day Gascony to the city of Toulouse, thence through Languedoc to the port of Roussillon on the Mediterranean Sea.

Within two days after arriving in Roussillon, Joseph had been able to gain passage aboard a ship bound for Crete, with brief stops at Sardinia and Syracuse. On the day following his arrival at Crete, he obtained passage on the small vessel which now carried him toward the port of Joppa, in Palestine. From there he would walk to his home at Arimathea, thence later go to Jerusalem in time for the Passover.

Because of his wife's illness during the two previous years, Joseph had not been able to make this journey to Arimathea and

Jerusalem. He was now anxious to again be home. He savored the thought of again walking the blessed streets of David's city. His fathers had worshiped for generations in the old Temple, before it had been destroyed, but Herod the Great had rebuilt a magnificent New Temple and Joseph looked forward to celebrating the Feast of the Passover there. He was also anxious to again visit with family members during his planned stay in Palestine.

He had previously sent messages to Capernaum, in Galilee, to family members who resided there, and in Nazareth, informing them of his wife's illness, then again of her recent death. Anna was barely fifty years of age when she died. Now, Joseph desired to tell them in person about Anna's last days. She had spent them in reasonable comfort, reminiscing about her parents and grandparents, sharing memories and thoughts about her sister, two brothers, and their families. Anna's heart held a great fondness for her family.

Then, too, having been chosen as a lay member of the Sanhedrin, Joseph also had some perfunctory duties therein to attend. While the chief priest held Joseph's proxy when his vote was required on matters before the Sanhedrin, Joseph looked forward to personally participating in their debate of religious matters which might come before them, then casting his own vote in the decisions being made.

He would also be able check on some personal business matters regarding the metal trade in which he had been long engaged. These last two items, however, now held a much lesser importance for Joseph than they had in previous years. For the most part, he had turned the operation of his metal business over to his son, Bran, but Joseph could not help being concerned because hundreds of workmen and their families counted on him.

Some things may have forced a change in Joseph's life, but seeing the outline of those Palestinian hills now quickened the pulse of his heartbeat. In another three hours he would be in port and his feet would be on Palestinian soil.

Chapter 2 – News from Home

Recent letters from family members living in Palestine had conveyed to Joseph the exciting news of a new spirit that was now astir among the Jews throughout Palestine. That new spirit was being kindled by a young teacher called Jesus of Nazareth.

It was Anna's grandniece, Claudia, who had kept them so well informed about the social and religious interests now taking place in Palestine. Four years previously, Claudia had accompanied Joseph and Anna to England, spending a season at their home in Siluria. Claudia had returned with them to Palestine the following season, but she had corresponded with them regularly since her return, keeping them abreast of family news as well as providing them with a full account of other news and events as they happened. Her last letter had arrived only eight days after Anna's death.

Claudia's letters these past three years had related, among other things, and with her usual dramatic flair, how Jesus had turned water into wine at a Cana marriage festival. Everyone was astonished, wondering how such a feat could be so deftly accomplished in everyone's sight, with the secret of how he did it remaining undetected by those present. In other letters, Claudia told them amazing stories about Jesus healing sick people, lame people, blind people, and some people with leprosy. She spoke of Jesus possessing some strange, but wonderful, new power.

Claudia had written that Jesus was traveling the countryside with a small band of followers, adding that everywhere Jesus' little troupe went, hundreds of people would come to hear him speak and to be healed of their diseases. Anna always relished Claudia's letters, but Joseph of Arimathea was silently amused, thinking that Claudia's reports overly exaggerated those events. That would not be an unusual thing for Claudia to do because, after all, Jesus was her oldest brother, and she had always adored everything about him.

Still, Joseph could not help but wonder about Claudia's reports. In one letter, she wrote that her mother, Mary, had confided to her: "Claudia, I want you to know that your brother has truly been born of God to do some wonderful thing. No matter what happens, promise me that you will always believe this."

Joseph of Arimathea had long sensed, along with most of the family, that his grandnephew was destined to make a lasting impression among the people of Israel. He realized that Jesus, after his grandfather Heli, was now the rightful heir to the throne of David. Joseph was not certain just what that meant, given the current political situation. The ancient prophecies were themselves cloaked with a mystery which Joseph could not fully fathom, but he fully believed. He had always suspected, and hoped, that somehow there was a connection between those ancient prophecies and Jesus.

Joseph remembered that Jesus had been born under unusual circumstances. There had been some behind the closed door talk, which Anna had always managed to avoid sharing with him in full detail. He also knew that Jesus' parents had spent almost eight years in Egypt, going there as a means of protecting their young son from Herod the Great's order to destroy all the male children born near the time of Jesus' birth. They had remained in Egypt until after Herod's death, when it was safe to bring their son back home to Nazareth.

All these events happened just after Joseph and Anna had moved to their new residence in Siluria, England, taking with them their daughter, Pernardin. Their son, Bran, was born in Siluria the year after their arrival there.

Their trips to Palestine were not as frequent in those days, so they missed out on much of the family happenings. Joseph was kept very busy in those early days, organizing and providing for his workers, overseeing the excavation, smelting, and shipping of his metal products, as well as always being on the move in different places to promote and sell his products. The expansion of the business inherited from his father was full of hectic, intense filled days. However, Joseph remembered there were whisperings about Anna's sister Elizabeth's son, John. While Joseph did not know all the details, he had recently received news that John was dead; beheaded because of sedition against the government, or that was the news.

Whatever was happening, Joseph would soon be able to make inquiry and thusly discern these matters for himself.

But, for a moment, he half-chuckled to himself in amusement, wondering what Jesus' father, Joseph of Bethlehem, if he were still alive, would have said about all the events which were said to be taking place. Joseph of Arimathea thought that Joseph of Bethlehem was a really good person, a thoughtful, studious, and quiet man, but one who always seemed a bit hesitant to embrace the unusual or the adventurous. He seemed contented just to be involved in the family's construction business. Joseph of Bethlehem had now been dead nearly four years.

The construction company had been started by his wife Anna's father, Joseph of Bethlehem's grandfather, Matthan of Galilee, who, across the years had grown his small carpentry business into a major construction enterprise. Following Matthan's death, the company had been carried on by Matthan's two sons, Heli and Jacob.

After Jacob's death, his son Joseph of Bethlehem became the major partner of his uncle Heli. Two of Joseph's other sons, James and Joses, resided in Jerusalem and Bethany, respectively, but Joseph's other two sons, Simeon and Jude, along with two of Joseph's brothers, Matthew and Jonas, and a son of Matthew and a son of Jonas, continued to be involved in the family's very healthy business. Their uncle Heli continued to monitor the financial affairs of the company but was content to leave the day-to-day operation in the hands of these younger men.

Joseph of Arimathea's mind dwelt for a moment on how many of the older members of the family were now dead, and how the young ones, themselves now grown, was scattered in a variety of different ways. Where had all the time gone? It had so swiftly slipped away. Family gatherings would never again be the same, at least not as he had remembered and relished their gatherings.

Noticing the fluffy clouds tumbling across the horizon, the memory of a childhood poem fluttered through Joseph's mind, something he had learned at his own dear mother's knee: "O little cloud, where did you come from? You were not, but now you are. You seem to ride on the roving winds as one does with the changing times. You cannot be measured, or weighed, or placed in a box, yet none can deny the value of your existence. O little cloud, where did you come from? You will cease to be, still you were here, and you made a difference in untold ways."

He also recounted the words of a favorite poem: "Blessed are our memories of family and kin, loved ones we once held here; now gone like day gives way to night, but for whom our love is cherished dear."

Caught up, as he was in his reverie, Joseph of Arimathea failed to notice the passage of time and distance until the small ship was within the outer reaches of the harbor at Joppa. Rising to his feet, identity papers in hand, Joseph anxiously readied himself for debarkation. He had arrived home three weeks before the Passover.

Chapter 3 – Signs of Promise

After spending the first night in Joppa, Joseph of Arimathea realized that he was not as indefatigable and resilient as he had once been. Fifty-three years of arduous responsibility had taken its toll on him. At the Inn, in which he had often stayed before, his movements were measured as he prepared to pay a visit upon Ezra ben Guran, the manager of his metals import business in Joppa.

Checking the records of metals and coal products shipped from England into that port, and the distribution of ores and coal to various points throughout Palestine and the surrounding areas, Joseph found the ledger accounts were thoroughly accurate. He had surmised beforehand that would be the case. Ezra ben Guran had been in his employ for almost thirty years and he was much more than an employee; Joseph respected and trusted him like a brother.

Joseph also took advantage of the opportunity to inquire of Ezra ben Guran concerning events taking place in Palestine. He made arrangements to take the evening meal with ben Guran at a small inn by the seaside.

When the pleasantries were taken care of, Joseph said, "I have received some interesting stories from relatives in Galilee about an amazing young teacher in that place, Jesus of Nazareth, he is called. Have you heard about him?"

A broad smile swept across ben Guran's face as he placed his glass of wine on the table. He looked straight into the eyes of Joseph of Arimathea and replied, "Yes sir, I indeed have! You must know that he is the son of your wife's nephew, Joseph of Bethlehem."

"Yes," answered Joseph, "He is the one? Tell me what you have heard about him?"

"I have not only heard many wonderful things concerning him, I have heard him speak and I have witnessed some of his miraculous deeds."

After catching his breath, ben Guran continued, "Two years ago, I had occasion to be in Capernaum to attend some accounts which we have there, and I had opportunity to go, with others, to hear Jesus speak at a gathering just outside of town. Thousands of people were present. I have never before or since seen such a large gathering of people." ben Guran then added:

"Jesus spoke about temperance and love";

"He also spoke about the values of living an exemplary life";

"About the virtues of being considerate of others";

"About the joy of serving one another";

"And about the wisdom of making holy choices in all matters";

"All of this, Jesus said, was the will of God and pleased God."

"And, when he spoke of God as 'our Father,' there was something in the manner by which he referred to God as, 'our Father,' that somehow seemed to make God so personal, and so near."

"Well, after Jesus had finished speaking, many sick people sought him, begging him to have mercy upon them and, believe it or not, Jesus healed them all."

"Jesus attended each and every person, like a shepherd would tend a new born lamb, or a mother would lovingly care for her child."

"Softly and tenderly he healed everyone who sought him. I still do not understand how he did what he did, but I, myself, saw it and, although I do not know by what means such feats were accomplished, I know what I witnessed."

Without giving the wide-eyed Joseph a chance to ask a question about everything he had said thus far, ben Guran added further, "When evening came, some of Jesus' disciples wanted him to send the crowds away that they might, themselves, go into Capernaum and get something to eat."

"Instead of sending the crowds away, however, Jesus instructed his disciples to feed the people where they were."

"Of course, the disciples had no food for themselves, much less ten thousand people."

"You should have seen his disciples scurrying around, busying themselves in an effort to obey Jesus' instructions"

"Well, one of his disciples located a young boy with a little basket of bread loaves and fishes."

"He brought the boy and his basket before Jesus and I saw the most amazing thing take place."

"It was even more astonishing than the healing of sick people."

"I saw Jesus look into heaven, I saw him pray, and then his disciples began to hand people bread and fish from that small basket until every one of us had received something to eat."

"Do not ask me how this was accomplished, but I saw it, and I also ate my fill of bread and fish."

"Joseph, I still cannot comprehend what happened, but I believe it!"

"Indeed, Jesus possesses some wondrous power to perform these mighty things."

Then, ben Guran stopped speaking. Having released his feelings, he waited for Joseph of Arimathea to respond.

Joseph sat for a moment, in silence, then excused himself and retreated to the toilet.

He needed that brief reprieve to digest everything which ben Guran had told him.

He needed an opportunity to retrieve his wits from the far field into which they had just been cast. Joseph spent those moments to form some questions in his mind; questions which might help prepare him for his own encounter with his grandnephew.

When Joseph had returned to the table, he thanked ben Guran for the information he had shared with him, asking ben Guran how the people of Palestine felt toward Jesus.

Without hesitation, ben Guran related how, from all he had heard since that time, was that, "Jesus is considered to be a mighty prophet, even perhaps Elijah, or Elias, of another prophet returned to proclaim the glory of Almighty God in Israel."

I do know, "ben Guran continued, "the spirit among our people is the highest I have observed since Palestine has been occupied by the Roman government. There is something different in the way people walk, the manner in which they greet one another, and attendance at the Temple in Jerusalem and in every synagogue is the largest it had ever been."

I do not know if there is a correlation between this new hope and the messages of Jesus, but it is evident to me that everyone is now different."

Ben Guran added that Jesus was the main topic of conversation wherever people gathered. Accordingly, further reports of Jesus' teachings and his many miracles continued to circulate, and the latest reports stated that Jesus had even raised to life again a little girl who had died.

All this information swarmed, unchecked, through Joseph's otherwise logical mind and, leaning across the table he asked ben Guran, "Do you suppose he is the Promised One of whom the prophets spoke?" The longing in ben Guran's voice was evident when he replied, "I hope so!"

When Joseph inquired how the occupying Roman government was responding to all of this, ben Guran replied that he did not know, primarily because he nor anyone else that he knew had even considered the feelings of the Romans, and also because this was strictly a spiritual matter about which the Romans had no particular interest.

Following a second night's rest, a renewed Joseph of Arimathea was up at dawn and walking on the road that would take him to home to Arimathea, arriving there before the beginning of the Sabbath that evening.

Along the way, he had occasion to converse with others who were walking the in the same direction. All spoke highly of the teachings and miracles being ministered in the region of Galilee by the young teacher.

He encountered two couples who informed Joseph they were on their way to Galilee to see and hear the one whom they described as, "the young and fearless prophet of God" of whom they had heard such marvelous things.

Joseph spent the next two days at his estate, located just outside the small village of Arimathea. It felt good to be home once more. It was a place which provided warm memories of times past. He was most happy to spend time again with his younger brother, Ely. Ely's wife, Orpah, was a delightful person to be around and she laid a feast for their evening meal. Joseph and Ely had a sister who lived in Bethsaida, in Galilee, but Ely had remained on their father's estate and managed its affairs.

It was the beginning of the Sabbath, but when the servants of their estate heard that Joseph had arrived home, they came at once and were most joyous to see him. It pleased Joseph that everything had been maintained in the best of order since he was last there. He longed to remain several days in that place, but Arimathea lay away from the normal travel routes whereby news could be passed along, therefore, neither his brother nor their servants had much to share concerning Jesus. Therefore, after two days, Joseph determined his need to go to Jerusalem was most urgent. He took with him a servant named Elizar, who was recommended by his brother.

It was in Jerusalem, after Joseph had arranged for living quarters during their stay there, and at the same time renting the large banquet hall in which to entertain family members and friends who he thought would join with him in celebrating the Passover. His lease was for a term of three months, with the facilities located near Herod's Palace in the Lower City section of Jerusalem. The landlord was a dear friend, and Joseph had often leased living quarters from him.

It was in Jerusalem that he initially encountered some despairing remarks about Jesus. This occurred on the second day following his arrival in Jerusalem, when Joseph went to the Temple of Solomon and renewed his acquaintance with Caiaphas, who was the high priest that year.

Before Joseph could make inquiry of him concerning Jesus of Nazareth, Caiaphas was already telling Joseph, "We have a problem which is causing we members of the Council grievous concern."

"There is a man in Galilee who is driving us to distraction, an upstart and self-proclaimed teacher of whom none of us has ever heard."

"The Council has had him investigated and the report tells us his name is Jesus, and that he is originally from Nazareth. You know what they say about that place; 'Can anything good come out of Nazareth?'"

"The report relates that this man has the people mesmerized with all manners of illusions and tricks; that they believe everything he tells them, and they flock from all over by the thousands to hear him speak."

Continuing his tirade, Caiaphas snorted, "I'll wager the man doesn't even know what the inside of a synagogue looks like, much less the Great Temple here in Jerusalem."

Hearing that outburst from Caiaphas, Joseph of Arimathea shelved his questions and said nothing. Privately, however, Joseph thought to himself how obvious is was that Caiaphas did not know that his wife Anne and her family constituted most of the residents of Nazareth.

Caiaphas's slur about Nazareth revealed again those ancient jealousies borne in the Jews who, for one reason or another, but mostly for imaginary reasons, had detested the royal descendants of David for generations. It was such pity that kind of divisive spirit had become a natural way of life for too many of them.

However, such a tirade from the mouth of the high priest meant that Joseph would have to be very careful in his effort to discover and discern for himself the truth about those things concerning Jesus. After all, Caiaphas's outburst could really be a warning? A shot across the bow because, perhaps, Caiaphas did know that Jesus was Joseph's nephew? There was no way to tell at the moment, but Joseph realized a storm was being brewed.

If his nephew should be a charlatan, as Caiaphas seemed to think, Joseph would try and find a way to call Jesus again to that accountability which Joseph remembered as the very hallmark of Jesus' character.

On the other hand, should Caiaphas and other members of the Sanhedrin be unjust in their judgment of his grandnephew, as he suspected they might be, Joseph would see if there was some way he might steer their hearts into a more favorable position regarding Jesus.

In any case, either task to broker any degree of reconciliation might likely prove to be as difficult as walking on water.

In the meantime, Joseph decided, the last thing he should do was to prematurely take sides and lock the door before he could get it open. Thus, it was his decision to be silent and be vigilant until he had gotten all of the facts straight.

Chapter 4 – In Pursuit of Truth

Lying in bed that night, Joseph finally drifted to sleep with thoughts about Jesus still churning in his mind. One thing he had decided upon, however, was to find James, the brother of Jesus, and talk with him. Joseph knew that James was living somewhere in Jerusalem, and it should not be too difficult to locate him. Always one to be independent, James had left the family firm and branched out on his own.

As luck would have it, when Joseph went to the Temple the following morning he spotted James sitting on the other side of the altar from him. When morning prayers had ended, Joseph made his way across the courtyard and caught James as he was leaving by a different door, one which led to the porch of the Temple.

The two men had never really been close to each other, James being the sort of person who seemed to live apart and in his own world. However, the usually somber James was genuinely enthusiastic to see his uncle Joseph. He was literally dancing as they affectionately embraced.

Strolling to a small, nearby shop, where they took refreshment, Joseph of Arimathea inquired of James about his mother and other members of his family. James responded, first, by telling his uncle the latest news about each person, where they were, what they were doing, reporting positively about their general health and happiness.

Joseph of Arimathea listened patiently as James catalogued for his uncle a litany of facts about their lives; all accept Jesus. James left the subject about his older brother for last, and leaning across he asked his uncle, "Have you heard about Jesus?"

Joseph related everything he had heard, including that scalding attack upon Jesus made by Caiaphas, the high priest.

Having related that information to James, Joseph of Arimathea concluded his response to James' question by saying, "That is why I wanted to see you, James. Being the brother of Jesus, I was hoping that you might provide me with your point-of-view about him."

Joseph of Arimathea waited as James framed, in his own mind, his personal and secret thoughts concerning Jesus. James couched his response with his overarching view of the religious and political situation of the long divided kingdom, Israel and Judah. Anything new had to be considered within the framework of an ancient background.

That view embraced those ancient quarrels between those Jews long aligned against the House of David, of which Jesus, James and their uncle Joseph belonged; the Hasmoneas blood lines; the Zadokite or Sadducean priests; plus the faction of Herod Antipas, tetrarch of Galilee.

Herod Antipas was a son of Herod the Great by his Samaritan wife, Malthace. He was, therefore, half Idumaemite (an Edomite) and half Samaritan. He had attempted to forge his ancestry to make it appear he was descended from the House of David and was, therefore, not only a ruler appointed by Caesar, but that his rule was according to the Law and the Prophets. Herod did this in an effort to fool the Galilean Jews, thus gaining from them a more favorable acceptance.

James then informed his uncle Joseph, "My cousin John, known as the Baptist, called Herod's hand about this and, in retaliation, Herod banished John from Galilee."

"John departed Galilee, going into exile across Jordan, in the wilderness of Decapolis," James said, "where he was able to continue preaching and baptizing. Always moving along the banks of the Jordan river, John eventually traveled all the way to Bethany-beyond Jordan, in Perea."

"The feud between John and Herod continued with each upstaging the other, until John publicly accused Herod of committing adultery with Herodias, his brother Philip's wife."

"Herod had John arrested for sedition and imprisoned in his fort at Machaerus. Sometime later he ordered John beheaded, and then had John's severed head delivered to Herodias, on a serving tray."

"John's death had sent shockwaves throughout the Jewish community because the people believed that John was a prophet sent by God."

"Upon learning of John's death, the people were disheartened, having lost the one whom they had hopes would lead them; although John always told them that the person would be someone other than himself; that his task was to prepare the way for the one who was the anointed of God."

"Following John's death," James continued, "Jesus emerged into the limelight and those who had followed John began following Jesus. Many others, coming from everywhere, flocked to join their numbers."

"How is your brother managing the situation with Herod?" Joseph asked.

"From what I hear," James replied, "Jesus has avoided any entanglement with Herod, being wise to stay clear of the trap that snared John."

"However, from what I have also overheard," James added, "There are others, long-standing enemies of our family, who are seeking ways to discredit and destroy the public image Jesus."

"Do you know who these people are?" Joseph asked.

"There are two groups," James responded, "one being the Sadducees, those members of the Zadokite party who inherited their priesthood from the prophet Zadok, but the second and more dangerous of the two groups, is the Pharisees."

James briefly catalogued for his uncle the second groups noble history, categorizing their founders as, "Valiant men whose religious conviction has uplifted for us the doctrines of fore-ordination and free will; the immortality of the soul; the resurrection of the dead; judgment, reward, and punishment accordingly as people have lived their lives; a place of sheol for the wicked and a place of grace for the faithful."

"But," James continued, "those today who rule the Pharisee party are mainly politicians and lawyers; vicious, self-righteous men who, as I see it, trivialize the law of Moses and institute their own rules."

"They have used their position on the Sanhedrin to establish a large number of required observances which are not written in the law of Moses, and they are more concerned about enforcing minute points and interpretations of the elders, or rulings which they themselves have introduced, than they are of encouraging people to embrace the original laws of Moses."

"In effect, Uncle Joseph, as I see it, the multitude of minuscule rulings by the Sanhedrin concerning the methods of our observing the traditions established by the elders actually tend to cut away and destroy the very heart of God's grace and man's free-will."

"They have also denounced John because he preached God's forgiveness for the repentance of sins. I am beginning to understand that John was entirely correct, because repentance comes from the heart of the sinner and forgiveness is grace which comes from the heart of God."

"However, the teachings of the Pharisees leave the heart of God and the heart of the people completely out of it. They say that God's grace is reserved solely for those whose obedience is to the external traditions and customs as defined and directed by the interpretations of the Sanhedrin."

Realizing that James had vented some serious issues, which most likely had been locked within him for months or longer, and knowing that the usually reserved James had probably said more in the last twenty minutes than in the past two months, Joseph of Arimathea reached across the table to touch his nephew's arm and said, "You do realize, James, that we are both Pharisees."

Joseph noted the questioning look on James' face as he replied, "Yes, but not like that!"

Joseph assured James by repeating his statement, "Yes, James, we are not like that, thanks be to God! Still, you have not yet told me about your brother."

"Jesus is in Galilee," James said. "He has gathered unto himself a sizeable number of men as his disciples, including James and John, the sons of my mother's sister Salome and her husband Zebedee. The others who follow my brother seem to be a questionable group. They include two brothers who are fishermen, named Simon and Andrew."

"There are also men named Philip, Nathanael, a tax collector named Levi, and a zealot named Simon. I do not recall at this moment the names of the others, but they are likely as infamous as the others. They all follow Jesus wherever he goes, and everywhere he goes large crowds of people gather to hear him speak and see his miracles of healing."

"Last winter, I visited with my brother when he came to the Feast of Dedication. I had thought that his coming to Jerusalem was to reveal himself as 'the anointed One' sent to reestablish the throne of David's line. But he did nothing to indicate that was his reason for coming here."

"We were walking and talking in Solomon's Colonnade of the Temple, and a crowd was following us everywhere, watching and waiting to see what Jesus would do. Finally, they began questioning him, taunting him to say something or do something beyond the ordinary. They asked, 'How long will you keep us guessing? If you are the One anointed of God, why not tell us? Don't keep us in suspense.'"

"Jesus' reply was, 'If I did tell you, you would not believe me. The miracles I have performed should speak to you, but you do not believe them. If I told you, neither would you believe me?'"

"When a few in the crowd became more insistent, Jesus explained how a shepherd knows his sheep and his sheep know their shepherd. Then he said, 'I have not delivered a message to you or performed any miracles for you because you are not my sheep and you will never recognize my voice or the miracles I perform.' "

"Then, looking in my direction, as if to answer some inquiries I had asked of him, Jesus added, 'My father, who is greater than all, has given my sheep to me and no one can steal them away from my Father, because I am my Father are one. It is for this that I have come into the world.'"

"I did not, at the time, grasp the meaning of Jesus' choice of words. No sooner had he spoke those words to them, however, when three or four voices in the crowd shouted in unison, 'Blasphemy! Blasphemy! He has committed blasphemy! Stone him! Stone him!' Having stones in their pockets as if prepared for the occasion, they began to throw the stones at him, but in the confusion Jesus managed to evade their attack and slipped away."

"Dear Uncle, I recognized two of the men who were taunting Jesus. They are associates of one of the Pharisees who sits with the Sanhedrin. And it was they who threw the rocks."

"I am convinced that the whole affair was rigged from the beginning as a means to discredit Jesus; the questioning, the taunting, the shouts of 'blasphemy;' and the stones in their pockets. Somehow, from the outset, I believe Jesus recognized their purpose, and the evil that were in their hearts."

"This is why I have suspicions about the Sanhedrin, and particularly the Pharisees. I have since met with my other three brothers, and we agree that we must now go to Jesus and persuade him to leave Galilee and come to Judea, to enter Jerusalem, and to announce to the Hebrew people his kingship and his reestablishment of David's throne."

"I feel certain Jesus is the One to whom John the Baptist referred, and I am equally certain that the majority of Hebrews will rise up and follow him. This is why I am so pleased you are here. Your presence, dear Uncle, is surely another sign of God that the time is now." A wide smile swept across the face of James as he made that last remark.

Joseph was stunned! Jesus, King of Judah and Israel? The country reunited? These were most pleasing thoughts, but there were also other considerations. What would they do about the Roman army? There were only light garrisons scattered through that geographical region at the present time, but the full force of Rome could be present within days.

A rebellion would be very bloody, and the outcome was uncertain. Yet, had not God raised up young Gideon to smite and defeat the powerful Midianites? Was the Great "I Am" about to install a second Moses? What James had said was very titillating – and, perhaps, disastrous.

Before going any farther, Joseph would have to carefully think about everything James had said. And, he certainly knew that he must speak with Jesus. Joseph had always been a person of faith, but at the moment he felt like a great knife was slicing his soul.

Chapter 5 – Joy in Believing

James had said that Jesus was in Galilee, so Joseph of Arimathea was up at dawn on the next day. Shortly thereafter he was on the way to find Jesus. The Sabbath would begin the next day and Joseph longed to attend Sabbath services in the Temple, but his finding Jesus was more urgent.

Most of the Jews traveled to Bethany, then cross the Jordan river at Jericho, or take the road leading to Bethany-beyond Jordan, then traveled upstream on the western side of the Jordan river. This route was chosen to avoid traveling through the country of the hated Samaritans.

Joseph held no such compulsion about going through Samaria because, after all, his home was located in the western region of Samaria, although not on the route he was taking.

Accompanied by Elizar for his traveling companion, they walked for a time in silence, Joseph's thoughts centered again on his home at Arimathea. It was located just outside the small town of Arimathea. Then, he began asking Elizar questions about a hundred things and happily discovered that his servant was most knowledgeable about everything he could think to ask.

"I have been away too long," he said. "Perhaps I can persuade Jesus to come and visit me at Arimathea." "We will not be interfered with during our conversations," he reasoned to himself. And, he thought about the many things he wanted to inquire of Jesus about. "Indeed, I will find him and I will invite him to come with me to Arimathea. That is what I will do," Joseph muttered to himself.

"Sir, what did you say?" asked Elizar.

"Nothing, really. I was only talking to myself," Joseph replied.

They spent the first night in a field just outside the small village of Shamir, then reached Bezek where they found a small inn in which to stay the second night. Since it was beginning of the Sabbath, they attended prayers with others in the inn, remaining in Bezek until the Sabbath had ended.

They rose early on the first day of the week, arriving at Beth-shean before noon on their fourth day's journey. There, Joseph learned that Jesus and his followers, two days previously, before the Sabbath began, were seen traveling south on the Jordan River road toward Jerusalem. Since it was beginning to storm, Joseph and Elizar agreed it was best to take refuge in the inn there, where they remained the rest of that afternoon and night.

Rising early the next morning, they were greeted with the fresh scent of a world washed clean by the rain. The sky was clear and the world looked beautiful in the morning sun as Joseph and his companion headed south along the Jordan River road. They set a fast pace in their desire to catch up with Jesus before he reached Jerusalem. With a large entourage, Joseph hoped Jesus would be moving at more a leisurely pace.

They walked a strong twenty miles and, fatigued to the point of exhaustion, spent the night with a family, opposite Succoth, across the Jordan River. The ache in Joseph of Arimathea's bones slowed their departure and first steps southward on the next day, but by midmorning they were almost back to their pace of the day before. By early evening they had reached the village of Auja, and decided to spend the night in that place.

In Auja, they were told that Jesus had passed that way in the afternoon of the previous day. They swiftly walked the five miles to the village of Gilgal on the next morning, where Joseph learned Jesus had only that morning departed. Those who lived in Gilgal were much stirred up by the sight of Jesus, proclaiming him to be, "A mighty prophet of God." Although tired from his journey, Jesus had spoken and many of the townspeople were healed of many kinds of illness. Joseph was told that, "Jesus and his followers left on the road to that leads to Jericho and Jerusalem."

Thus, it was that afternoon, just beyond Jericho, where Joseph of Arimathea found his grandnephew, Jesus. He was speaking and his followers, which included many citizens from Jericho, were gathered by the hundreds in a large field which a farmer had lent for Jesus to use. Listening intently, Joseph recorded in his journal what Jesus was saying:

"He who was in the form of the Father took the form of man. He who was made in the likeness of the Father was made in the likeness of man. He who was of the Father and the Spirit was made flesh. He who was in the beginning equal with the Father and the Spirit became creature and servant. He became man, and when he became man, he was man as really as he was of the Father."

"In order to redeem man from what man is, he was made what man is. Man is flesh and the Son was made flesh. Man is under the law and the Son was made under the law. Man is sold in sin and laden wit iniquity, and the Father has lain on his Son the iniquity of all men. The Son became flesh in order that man, who is flesh, might become Spirit and be reconciled to the Father."

"The Son, who was altogether of the divine nature, was made to partake of human nature in order that all who are altogether of human nature might be partakers of the divine nature. In this, the Father, who is full of grace and forgiveness, hath bestowed on all men the free choice to receive unto themselves the divine nature of their heavenly Father."

"You have seen how in times of tragedy, want and need, man has overcome his pain, hurt, hate and fear. To overcome these troubles, man has arrived at a place of reconciliation by choosing to rise above his troubles. You must now also find room in your heart to reconcile with your neighbor, even those who are your enemies."

"You cannot reconcile where there is hatred. Nor can you be reconciled by a sword, nor where there is dominion over another. Yet, where there is love, you can be reconciled with one another, just as I and my Father are reconciled to each other. I have in me, and it is the hope of my Father, that you will learn to fall in love again. And, just as I and my father love you, there can be nothing in your heart that is greater than my Father's love, for I and my Father are love. This is the message you are to write on your heart, and on your neighbor's heart, that together you may have the blessings of my Father and I."

Then, Jesus bade those who were sick or diseased to, "Come and be healed that all might see and believe the wondrous love and power my Father has given to me for your benefit." Joseph recorded that, by his count, Jesus healed more than three hundred people that afternoon.

Joseph also noted that, after Jesus had finished, the disciples sent the people away that they might go into Jericho and refresh themselves, saying Jesus would speak again that evening if they returned and desired to hear him.

Joseph saw that Jesus was walking away, in the opposite direction, and he started after him when someone held out both arms, as if to stop him from going any farther, saying, "The Master must have his rest now. Come again this evening."

Pulling up short, Joseph said, "Would you tell your Master that his granduncle, Joseph of Arimathea, is here and wishes to see him? I have traveled a very long way to see my grandnephew again."

Telling Joseph to wait until the message was delivered to his Master, the man departed in the direction taken by Jesus. Later, Joseph would learn his name was Philip. Within a few minutes, Joseph saw his grandnephew running across the field from the direction in which he had previously disappeared, his hair and robe blowing in the breeze, and both arms outstretched as he ran to where Joseph of Arimathea was standing. Their clasp of each other was long and affectionate as they kissed one another on first one check, then the other. No words were required until, after several moments, Jesus stepped back and smiled at his Uncle Joseph with deep affection.

An obviously excited Jesus then asked question after another, "Tell me, dear Uncle, how did you find me? Where have you come from? Where is Aunt Anna? How does it go with Parnardin and Bran? Have you traveled long? You must be weary? Do you need to rest? May I give you something to eat? Forgive me for not giving you opportunity to speak, but it is such a joy to see you again, dear Uncle."

After introducing his servant, Elizar, to Jesus, they began walking in the direction from which Jesus had come. Joseph informed Jesus of Anna's death, explaining the reason for his not being able to be in Palestine the past two years. Joseph also provided Jesus with the latest news concerning his children, Penardim and Bran, about whom Jesus had inquired.

Joseph then said, "Your sister, Claudia, wrote to us that you were speaking and doing many wonderful deeds. I thought perhaps she exaggerated somewhat. Since my arrival in Palestine, many have informed me of your work. I have also talked with James."

"I arrived here just as you finished speaking, and I saw with my eyes the miracles of healing which you performed. You have indeed been gifted with power that is beyond mortal man, for I have seen the glory of Almighty God at work through you."

"Are you the One?"

They had reached a small shelter that had been sat up as a place for Jesus and his Apostles, as Jesus introduced them, to rest for a time from the work they were doing. Following introductions of those present, Jesus bade his Uncle to sit, while one of his Apostles entertained Elizar by escorting him to some refreshments.

"Am I the One?" Jesus said, repeating his uncle's question?

With a twinkle in his eye, Jesus returned the question to his uncle, "Are we not all the One?"

"Is not every person who does fully the will of my Father, the One?"

"Was not Moses the One?" Jesus asked?"

"Was not Gideon the One?"

"Were not each of the prophets, in their time, the One?"

Joseph of Arimathea remembered this little stratagem used by his grandnephew when he wanted to avoid making a direct response. Jesus could go on forever, by answering one question with another question without revealing anything one way or another. Now, he was doing it again.

"Dear Jesus," Joseph said, "Do not speak to me in riddles. Speak to the heart of an old man who has always loved you, and loves you now most dearly like my own son."

"Your brother, James, thinks you are the One sent by God to reestablish the throne of David's line, and the whole nation awaits your coming to Jerusalem to make that announcement. Others say that you are the One, as a great prophet, sent by God, and they will follow you wherever you lead them, as their ancestors followed David."

I, myself, along with members of your family, have always believed you were marked by birth for a great purpose, to glorify Almighty God and to save God's people. I cannot imagine what that entails, but let me ask you straight, "Jesus, are you God's Messiah?"

Jesus smiled at Joseph for a long time then, speaking softly, said, "Yes! I am he!"

Joseph of Arimathea had thought so, but Jesus' response was so completely sincere that Joseph was taken aback and knew not what else to say. It was as if he had knowingly stepped off of solid ground into an unfathomable abyss of holiness, knowing not what to do or say beyond the moment.

Joseph sat there for the longest time, looking into the face of a smiling Jesus. It was a "kuros" moment. Then, driven by a sudden impulse, Joseph of Arimathea clasped the hands of Jesus within his own hands and, bending low, kissed the hands of Jesus, exclaiming, "My Lord and my God!"

After a few moments, when Joseph had regained his composure, Jesus said, "I am taking my Apostles to Jerusalem, to celebrate the Passover. There, the people will see me."

Joseph of Arimathea relayed the information provided to him by James, and also told Jesus about the outburst and slur made against him by Caiaphas, the high priest.

Jesus replied, "Those who live in darkness are constantly stirred in their hearts by the suspicion of some fear or hatred. It is when men begin to think they have the right to judge and punish others in God's holy name, or when they feel it is necessary to defend God because God is somehow incapable of defending himself, that they tend to commit the worst kinds of evil. It is a condition of the heart inherited from their fathers. It blights their soul, and they will not break the chain to set themselves, and their children, free from their slavery of the heart; that they may believe, be forgiven, be reconciled, and be healed."

"I must go to Jerusalem in order that the scriptures be fulfilled. Those who would judge and kill me cannot destroy me. They have the earthly power to kill the body, but they have no power to kill the soul. My Father' has power that is greater than the power of this world, and he will raise me again on the third day; that all may see and believe that I am in the Father and he is in me. Tell James that I am not of this world, and my kingdom is not of this world."

"My kingdom is an everlasting kingdom into which all may enter, even my enemies, if they repent and believe in me. Neither the evil in the heart of man nor death by the hands of man can lay claim to victory, because victory belongs to my Father who is in heaven.

I have come from my Father, that all men may repent of their evil ways and be reconciled in love to my Father, and to one another. If they repent and are reconciled in love to my Father, they are also reconciled to me, for my Father and I are one."

Then, Jesus added, "Go and tell this to Caiaphas, and tell the leaders of the Council, that they shall see in Jerusalem the power and the glory of God's love raised up."

Having said that, Jesus excused himself, for he needed to refresh himself before speaking again that evening, but informing his uncle that, after staying the night in Jericho, on the next day he was going to the home of Lazarus, in Bethany, where he would remain for the Sabbath. He invited his uncle to again join him there.

Joseph of Arimathea found Elizar, his servant and traveling companion. Joseph would have remained to hear Jesus speak again, but sensed something in the tone of Jesus' voice directing him to go on to Bethany. Joseph said nothing to Elizar concerning those things Jesus had told him. When they arrived at Bethany, Joseph sent Elizar ahead to Jerusalem, while finding quarters at an inn for himself. There, he awaited the arrival of Jesus the following day.

Chapter 6 – O Jerusalem

It was at noontime when the crowds began arriving in Bethany. To the people of Jerusalem they exclaimed, with excited voices, that Jesus of Nazareth would soon arrive. They also related, to any person who would listen, that Jesus had only that morning, as he was departing Jericho, restored the sight of a man who had been blind since birth. "Bartimaeus," they said, "was the blind man's name."

Shortly thereafter, the main body of Jesus' followers, with Jesus in the lead, came into view. He spoke for a brief time, but Joseph of Arimathea could not position himself close enough to hear what Jesus was saying. Afterwards, the crowd began to break into small groups, each wandering their own way, while Jesus and his Apostles headed in a different direction. That was the direction in which Joseph also proceeded.

Seeing Jesus to into a house, Joseph made his way through the small crowd still standing outside and was pleased that Philip, to whom he had been introduced the day before, was expecting him. Philip immediately ushered Joseph into the house. Jesus was seated when Joseph entered the house, but arose to greet his granduncle with warm affection, then bid him set next to him.

There were several others in the room and, in addition to Lazarus, they consisted mostly of his Apostles, but not all of them. The sisters of Lazarus, named Martha and Mary, were there too. The two women were seeing to everyone's comfort and busy preparing and serving the meal. It was during the meal that Joseph learned that Lazarus was one of those persons whom Jesus had restored to life after he had died.

Lazarus was reclining on a pillow across the table from Jesus, smiling, eating, and looking none the worse for having experienced death. He seemed as natural in his appearance as every other person at the table. Inwardly, Joseph of Arimathea would have liked to ask him a hundred questions, but he was loath to do so. In fact, the presence of Lazarus had a squelching effect on Joseph's desire to do anything which might identify him as "out of place."

After the meal, as the others were engaged in small groups of conversation, except Joseph, who was content to be quiet and observe their proceedings, Mary entered the room and seated herself beside Jesus. Joseph watched as she opened an exquisite jar and poured its contents of expensive perfume onto Jesus' feet, then using her hair as a towel, wiped Jesus' feet. Suddenly, one of the Apostles began to scold Mary. He was concerned about Mary's lavish use of such a costly perfume. Joseph wondered why he was so concerned, it was not his perfume and Mary's lavish use of it was without consequence or cost to that Apostle. In fact, Joseph thought Mary's actions displayed an act of profound generosity and devotion.

So did Jesus! He immediately chastised that Apostle for having scolded Mary and, in turn, thanked Mary for what she had done. To others in the room, Jesus said, "Mary has anointed my feet in preparation for the day of my burial." The Apostle whom Jesus had chastised for his unkind remarks to Mary appeared angry, while the others soon returned to their former conversations.

Using that as an opportunity to excuse himself, Joseph prepared to leave the house, but Jesus caught him at the door, in a gesture of bidding him farewell. Stepping outside for a moment, they found that a large crowd had gathered before the house. They quickly reentered the house and Jesus said, "When you go to Jerusalem, tell the members of the Council that the kingdom of Heaven is at hand. Ask them to open their hearts and embrace that which my Heavenly

Father is sitting in their midst." With that said, Jesus clasped his uncle to his breast, then returned to his place and his companions at the table.

It was still early, and there was still enough time to be in Jerusalem before the Sabbath began. Joseph started immediately, traveling across the Mount of Olives and down its slope into Jerusalem.

By the time Joseph of Arimathea arrived at his quarters, he thought that it had been one of those days which tries the soul of man. It had, in fact, been a full week and, being exhausted, hungry as he was, he fell immediately to sleep.

It was midmorning before he wakened. It was the Sabbath and, for the first time in ages, Joseph had missed early morning prayer. After their arrival in Jerusalem the previous evening, Elizar had located a small shop nearby where he obtained something for them to eat and, after dressing and eating the prepared meal, Joseph went immediately to the Temple.

Joseph was looking for some of his fellow members of the Sanhedrin. He hoped to engage them in conversation about Jesus of Nazareth and share with them some of the insight about him that he had gained. He reasoned to himself that if they would listen to what Jesus asked him to tell them, he could then persuade them to go with him to meet Jesus in person, where their opinion of Jesus, unlike that of Caiaphas, might be changed. Even if some of them could band together, they might avert any premature opposition to Jesus by the entire Sanhedrin.

Three members of the Sanhedrin whom Joseph approached had already followed the lead of Caiaphas and closed their minds concerning Jesus of Nazareth. No amount of persuasion could change their hearts. However, Joseph was able to otherwise convince three others, named Gamaliel, Nichodemus, and Simon to maintain open minds in regard to Jesus.

Like Joseph, these three were lay members of the Sanhedrin, selected because of their prominence within the Jewish community more than for their ability to interpret the laws instituted by the

Sanhedrin, Gamaliel being an exception. He was a teacher of the law and his advice on matters was constantly sought to guide other members in their interpretation of the law.

Nichodemus was a successful merchant in all manners of wares and goods, having a trade route which regularly took him throughout the area of Judea, as well as Galatia, Greece, Corinth, and Macedonia. He also had a previous encounter with Jesus, ever since being intrigued by Jesus' telling him of a new birth. Since Nichodemus was often absent from Palestine and meetings of the Sanhedrin, his proxy vote was held by the high priest, like that of Joseph's vote.

Simon, too, had previously met Jesus when a sinful woman of the town where he lived entered his house as he and Jesus were taking a meal. Weeping, she had wet Jesus' feet with her tears, dried them with her hair, than poured perfume on the feet of Jesus. Simon thought that if Jesus were a prophet, he should have recognized the woman was a sinful person. However, Jesus took the occasion to teach Simon an important lesson about judgement and forgiveness; for after forgiving the woman's sinfulness, Jesus blessed her and told the woman to go in peace.

These were the three men whose hearts and minds were more open, along with Joseph, and together they might be able to convince the remaining members of the Sanhedrin to be patient and tolerant of Jesus following his arrival into Jerusalem; to avoid a clash which would do no party any good, rather could cause great harm to many; to set aside all that which they had heard concerning Jesus until they could see and judge him on his own merits, because, as Gamaliel would later caution all members of the Sanhedrin when they actually met, "This could be the work of Almighty God and we must be careful not to oppose God, or the One whom God sends to us. So let us be alert and be aware lest we shame ourselves and the people."

When Joseph of Arimathea retired for the evening, he prided himself for having accomplished his goal. That small group of prestigious men might help bring some degree of patience and wisdom to other members of the Sanhedrin, many of whom had already made up their minds to cast Jesus in a negative light. The rest of the Sanhedrin would not dare to go completely against them.

The Sabbath ended, it was midmorning when crowds of people began swarming into Jerusalem, coming from Bethany and descending from the Mount of Olives. Joseph hurried to meet them, for Jesus was coming and he wanted to tell Jesus of his success and the plans to meet with the Sanhedrin that evening.

What Joseph encountered, however, was a parade of Jesus' followers chanting his arrival with shouts of praise and placing their cloaks and extra garments onto the street where Jesus was to arrive. When people on the street made inquiry about what they were doing, they were told that Jesus, the prophet from Nazareth, was coming. Word of his impending arrival spread quickly among the people, many having previously heard about the mighty miracles which Jesus had wrought, thus hundreds of people begin stripping the branches from palm trees and waving them, marched forth with loud acclaim, to greet Jesus.

When they saw him, riding down the street upon a small donkey, many in the crowd gasped. They were shocked, because such an appearance of one believed to be so great a prophet was disappointing in appearance. A great hush fell over most of the crowd, sending a deep hurt, like a well-aimed arrow, into Joseph's heart.

"Why a small donkey?" "What is Jesus doing?" "Does he not have any pride?" Many of the people who had rushed forth to welcome him began dropping their palm branches and walking away. They had expected much more. Only those who had led Jesus into Jerusalem continued the celebration. When Jesus passed by where Joseph was standing, the smile on his face made him look as if he were the Lord of the universe. Joseph thought sadly to himself, "This is such a ridiculous scene!"

The noisy, ragged army of people, with Jesus still riding the donkey, finally made their way to the Temple. Upon entering the courtyard of the Temple, Jesus began upending the tables of the money changers and those who sold doves to visitors that they might offer the doves as a sacrifice. The entire display was a rowdy scene and Joseph of Arimathea was absolutely dumbfounded.

"Certainly, those who traded within the Temple courts paid the Sanhedrin a handsome price for permission to set up their selling tables and, certainly, the space they occupied deprived the Gentiles of space which had originally been set aside for the Gentiles, but the behavior of Jesus was just as certainly uncalled for," thought a very disturbed Joseph of Arimathea.

"In ten minutes, he has undone everything I accomplished yesterday in his behalf," an incredulous Joseph muttered under his breath. "It will now be impossible for us to intercede with the other members of the Sanhedrin. And, most likely, also lost are the three votes I had gained."

Sure enough, when the Sanhedrin met later that evening, the behavior of Jesus in the Temple courtyard was the primary topic placed on the table of conversation and, neither he nor any of the other three were prepared to speak out in behalf of Jesus. The four of them sat quietly, listening to the others, and looking at the floor. Joseph knew that at the moment there was no way they could speak out in Jesus' favor, not after the inexplicable escapade of his overturning the tables of those traders in the Temple courtyard.

Joseph learned that Jesus and his Apostles, and many of his followers, had returned to Bethany for the night, but Jesus himself had stayed on the Mount of Olives with his disciples. Joseph walked slowly to his own quarters in the Lower City. Nichodemus walked with him, but they did not speak, each of them keeping their own thoughts to themselves.

On the following morning, when Joseph arrived at the Temple, he found Jesus and his followers already there. Joseph did not speak to Jesus at that time, but following morning prayer, Jesus began speaking to a large group that had gathered about him. Joseph moved to where he could hear Jesus speaking, but at the rear of those gathered.

Jesus was telling a parable of a landowner who engaged some tenants to live and work on his land. When the owner sent a servant to collect some fruit of the vineyard as payment for rent, the tenants decided to beat him and sent him away without any fruit. The landowner sent other servants but those tenants, likewise, shamefully beat and sent each servant away without any fruit as payment. Some servants the tenants went so far as to kill. Finally, the only person the landowner had left to send to collect some fruit as payment for rent was his son. Surely they will respect my son, the landowner thought, but the tenants conspired, agreeing with one another that if they killed the landowner's heir, they would thereby have the inheritance of the land for themselves. So they killed the landowner's son and threw his body out of the vineyard. What then will the landowner to? He will kill those tenants and give the vineyard to others. "Now, hear this scripture," said Jesus, "The stone the builders rejected has become the capstone; the Lord has done this, and it is marvelous in our eyes."

Someone from the other side of the crowd then shouted a question at Jesus. "By whose authority are you doing these things?" Another man shouted, "Who gave you authority to do this?" Joseph looked in the direction of the questioners and spotted three members of the Sanhedrin standing somewhat apart on the other side of the crowd.

Jesus countered the two questioners with a question of his own, "Answer my question, and I will tell you by what authority I am doing these things."

"John's baptism ~ was it from heaven or from men? Tell me!"

Joseph watched as the three huddled together for a few moments before admitting, "We don't know."

"Then," replied Jesus, "Neither will I tell you by whose authority I am doing these things."

Joseph smiled to himself. "Good for Jesus," he thought. Joseph didn't particularly care for those three members of the Sanhedrin, and he felt good by the manner in which Jesus had put them in their place. That repartee somewhat served to ease the tension in Joseph's heart over the episode of the upturned courtyard tables on the previous day.

Chapter 7 – A Time of Choices

At the evening meeting of the Sanhedrin, those same three members reported a completely different and distorted picture of Jesus' teaching that morning. Their hatred for Jesus was clearly evident. Finally, Joseph could no longer endure their outright falsification of that event and, speaking to the Sanhedrin, said, "I saw the whole thing myself, and what I saw was completely different from what you are saying. Tell us about your questions and the response that Jesus gave to you." Unknown to Joseph, Nichodemus had also been present when Jesus was speaking that morning. He also spoke up, questioning the veracity of those three and echoing Joseph's desire to have them relate their questions to Jesus, and his response to them.

They deflected the queries of Joseph and Nichodemus by shifting the topic in a different direction. Joseph now knew in his heart, however, that Nichodemus was a friend he could count on. He also knew that a nerve of uncertainty had been struck concerning Jesus. This emboldened Joseph to speak up in Jesus' behalf.

"Some of you are teachers of the law," Joseph began. "I, too, know the law, but I am not gifted to debate its finer points, so I leave the debate about the law to experts, such as you. Now, it has been said that I am an expert in my own field of endeavor, both a proven and a successful expert if I may humbly say so."

"Now there are times when I do not have in me the solution to some problems which arise. I often find myself having to confer with others to arrive at a solution to the problem. Ultimately, however, the decision in such matters rests entirely on my shoulders, and I am keenly aware that the livelihood of thousands of workers and their families can be adversely affected if the decision that I make should be wrong."

"I have also observed there are occasion when you who are experts in the law are required to make a decision. Sometimes, in that process, I have seen you in total disagreement with each other about something. To me, it indicates there are times when absolute answers to complex problems are elusive, unclear, uncertain, or as confusing to you in your field as they sometimes are to me in my field. But, during those struggles to seek truth, I have been encouraged by the manner in which you struggle to find a middle ground in order to arrive at a decision that is for the good of all."

"I suggest the issue concerning Jesus of Nazareth is one of those moments in which we should engage ourselves in such a struggle. Perhaps his behavior is not the way we would do things, and perhaps his teachings challenge the traditional ways in which we observe the law, but to dismiss him outright like a braggart or a thief may result in our doing great harm."

Continuing, Joseph said, "I have heard Jesus speak on several occasions, as have some of you. I am intrigued, as well as challenged, by what he teaches. It is possible that we do not yet have all the answers, just as some of you were unable to answer the question which Jesus asked of you today. He is not a Zealot, but speaks a message of love and reconciliation. I implore you to join with me, to unite, and to struggle together in understanding this man whom many believe is a prophet sent by God. What if he is a prophet? Are you unwilling to find out? What if he is our promised Messiah, the Son of God?"

When he had finished speaking, there was complete silence around the room. Finally, Caiaphas, the high priest, said: "If that is all, the meeting is adjourned until tomorrow night," a meeting which

Joseph of Arimathea would not attend. Joseph had spoken his heart and, for better or worse, he left them, individually and collectively, to forge their own choice concerning Jesus of Nazareth.

It was not until the next day that Joseph was able to relate all this information to Jesus. Joseph informed Jesus that, while some members of the Sanhedrin were looking for ways to discredit him, at least three other members had agreed to be fair minded, until the episode of the overturned tables of the money changers and traders two days previously. Joseph wanted to know why Jesus had exhibited that particular kind of behavior.

Jesus explained his actions "as the wrath of God," because those who permitted the traders to clutter the Court of the Gentiles were, by such approval, deliberately keeping the Gentiles away from the Temple; denying them space to attend and worship God. Jesus explained, "My Father long ago instructed the Hebrews they were chosen to be a light to the people of all nations that all people might come together in worship and fellowship. Instead of welcoming others, they have been disobedient by becoming high-minded and haughty toward my Father's other children."

Joseph said, "Yesterday, I listened as you talked about a landowner and his tenants who, when the landowner sent a servant to receive from the tenants the landowners share of fruit from the vineyard, but one servant after another the tenants beat and sent away empty handed. Some servants the tenants killed. When there were no more servants left to send, the landowner reasoned that his tenants would respect his son and heir, but the tenants conspired together and killed also the landowner's son. You said the landowner, himself, then went and killed those tenants and gave the land to others in their place."

Joseph added, "I think the story you were telling was a parable, but tell me if I am correct in interpreting its meaning. Is this story about us Jews, and our relationship to God?"

Jesus said, "You are correct in its meaning concerning the Jews. God is the landowner, because God created the heavens and the earth. Everything belongs entirely to him. The heir is his Son, who was with God when the heavens and the earth were created as a vineyard."

"The tenants are those who live in the vineyard which God created. They are the Hebrew children of God. Their task has been to produce fruit and share it with the landowner as payment for the privilege of living in God's vineyard."

"The fruit which the landowner expects his tenants to produce and share with him is the other nations and peoples of earth, those who have forgotten their source of existence and who do not know that God is also their Father. The tenants in my Father's vineyard were chosen and assigned the task of bringing the other peoples of earth to the table of love and fellowship. This is the fruit of their labors which my Father has desired, but this they have refused to do."

"The servants whom the landowner sends to the tenants are the prophets, those who down through ages past the Hebrews have rejected and sent away, empty handed. O how my Father and I would have gathered them together in love, as a mother hen gathers her brood under her wings, but they would not."

"Now, as the landowner, God has sent his Son to them, thinking they will surely respect and honor his heir. They each have a choice, either to respect the Son and at last give to him God's share of fruit from the vineyard in which they live, or to reject the Son and sent him, too, away empty handed."

"They may choose to kill the Son. They can kill his body but, him they cannot destroy because in three days my Father will raise the Son to life again, and you will see him, risen and alive in all his glory. But if they kill his body, my Father will come and remove them from his vineyard, and he will deny them as his people until they individually repent and change from their evil conspiracy to kill the Son and heir, and then be born anew from above. If they are born again they will be restored as members of a new people with whom

I and my Father will covenant; that all the nations and peoples may come together and share in mutual love and fellowship."

"My dear uncle, I tell you this now, because I and my Father are doing a new thing. When the Son is risen from the dead, he will show himself to his disciples, removing all worldly doubts and fears from their hearts. You, too, will see him, be filled with a new Spirit, and as his disciple you then know what you are to do."

"Now, I will celebrate the Passover with my disciples and I need a room here in Jerusalem where we can observe the Feast. Can you provide me such a place and will you come to the Feast?"

Joseph of Arimathea's mind was busy trying to absorb all that Jesus had just told him, almost missing the request made of him to supply a room in which to celebrate the Passover Feast. Then, Joseph remembered the large banquet hall he had obtained along with his living quarters, one in which he had hoped to entertain family members and friends. He had rented it for three months and, being located the Lower City section of Jerusalem, it would be the perfect place for Jesus and his disciples to meet. After telling Jesus the location of the banquet hall, telling him it had the amusing name of "The Upper Room," he assured Jesus that everything was in readiness.

After leaving Jesus in the Temple, Joseph of Arimathea returned to his quarters and began to make preparations of "The Upper Room" banquet hall for Jesus and his disciples. To Joseph's eye, when he entered the room, everything appeared to be in readiness for its use. "If only Anna were here," he thought, "She would know exactly what to do." Joseph missed his Anna, and loneliness swept across his heart for a few moments. Then, as if Anna had spoken to him, he said, "Cups! And plates! They will need cups and plates from which drink and eat during the Passover Feast!"

At dawn, Joseph woke Elizar, his servant and companion from Arimathea. After refreshing themselves Joseph headed toward the marketplace with Elizar in tow. After an hour search, they found a small store that had exactly what Joseph was searching. He purchased twenty finely crafted goblets and some small plates, along with one set of a larger, pure silver, chalice and plate. At another shop he purchased some candles and holders, and at another several additional pillows to place around the tables in the room. Then he found a shop where he arranged to obtain appropriate foodstuffs for the Passover Feast.

The following day passed without incident as Joseph made last minute preparations to celebrate the Passover Feast with Jesus and his disciples. Those who were present at the Passover Meal were Jesus and his twelve disciples, Mary the mother of Jesus, James his brother, Mary Magdalene, Joanna, and Mary the mother of James, in addition to Joseph of Arimathea and Elizar his servant. Elizar assisted the women with their serving while the men prepared to engage in the ritual prayers of the Passover.

After the meal was ended, Jesus said, "I have eagerly desired to eat this Passover with you before I suffer. I will not eat of it again until the kingdom of God is fulfilled."

Then Jesus took a small, unbroken loaf of bread from the silver tray before him, blessed the bread and said, "This is my body which is broken for you." Dividing the bread among them, he added, "Hereafter, when you eat of the loaf, do this in remembrance of me."

Likewise, he took the silver cup of wine and blessing it, he passed it among them saying, "This is my blood of the new covenant that I am about to make which is poured out for you and for many. Drink from this, all of you, in remembrance of me, for I will not drink of this fruit of the vine again until that day when I drink it anew with you in my Father's kingdom."

After this, Jesus got up from the meal, took of his outer garments, and wrapped a towel around his waist. Then, pouring water into a basin, he began to wash the feet of those in the room, then drying them with the towel that was around his waist. When he had finished, he explained what he had just done, saying, "If I, your Lord and Teacher, have washed your feet, you also should wash one another's feet. I have set you an example that you should do as I have done for you, for I tell you this truth, no servant is greater than his master, nor is the messenger greater than the one who sent him. Now that you know these things, you will be blessed if you do them."

After they sang a hymn, Jesus and his disciples went out to the Mount of Olives. The women, being exhausted, remained in The Upper Room, having been invited by Joseph of Arimathea to rest there for the night. Mary, the niece of Joseph and the mother of Jesus, appeared as if she could not take another step. James retired to his own quarters.

Joseph, always a generous and thoughtful host, and Elizar his servant, remained for a time in The Upper Room to see that the room was straightened up for the women to rest, and to see that the cups and plates which were used in the Passover Meal were cleaned and put away in Joseph's own quarters. Afterwards, leaving Elizar at the inn, Joseph of Arimathea departed for the Mount of Olives, to meet Jesus and his disciples in a grove of olive trees, as described to him by Jesus.

Chapter 8 – The Night of Horrors

When Joseph arrived on the Mount of Olive, becoming confused, he made a wrong turn which took him in a direction opposite than that he intended. When he realized his error, he retraced his steps back to the point of his error. On arriving there, he encountered a detachment of soldiers coming from Jerusalem, followed by a large crowd with torches and clubs. They were following one of the disciples of Jesus, named Judas Iscariot.

Walking with strident haste, the soldiers, followed by the crowd, quickly took that turn which Joseph had originally missed, moving on toward a grove of olive trees where Joseph now believed Jesus and his disciples had said they would be.

Joseph fell in behind the crowd and when he asked a man who was walking beside him at the rear of the crowd, "Where is everybody going with such haste?" The man replied, "I do not know where, but those in front asked me to come along and help them catch a breaker of laws; a thief I imagine."

Joseph thought to himself, "Perhaps I have again taken the wrong turn to where Jesus said that he and his disciples would be." However, when the crowd halted just inside a grove of olive trees, Joseph thought, "No! I am sure this is the place."

Voices at the front of the crowd rose above the others, indicating that some kind of commotion was taking place. In an effort to find out what was happening, Joseph began pushing his way toward the front. It was impossible to get very far, however, because others in the throng were also pressing forward. The pandemonium arising at the front of the crowd grew into a bedlam of shouting voices, but it was impossible to understand what was being said.

Joseph could do nothing except hold his position, squeezed, in the middle of the pack when, suddenly, he realized the crowd was beginning to break up, parting to each side to make way for someone from the front to pass through. Joseph was also in the process of stepping aside when he recognized Jesus, with his hands tied, being roughly shoved through the crowd by two soldiers, followed by other soldiers and some men who were holding clubs and torches.

Joseph began following, getting as close as he could manage to Jesus, and by the time they had returned Jesus to Jerusalem, and to Caiaphas' courtyard, Joseph was at the front of the crowd. A disciple of Jesus, the one Jesus called Peter, had also made his way to the front of the crowd and was now beside Joseph. They had arrested Jesus, but Peter did not know why they had done so, except someone had told him it was on orders from the Sanhedrin.

Because Joseph of Arimathea was known to the high priest, he was permitted to go with Jesus into the high priest's courtyard, but Peter was stopped and had to remain outside at the door. After receiving permission, Joseph went outside and, after speaking to the girl who was on duty there, took Peter into the high priest's courtyard with him. As Peter passed the girl at the door, she asked Peter, "Are you also one of this man's disciples?" Peter denied it and, moving away from Joseph, seated himself by the fire, where several soldiers were warming themselves.

First, the detachment of soldiers took Jesus before Annas, the father-in-law of Caiaphas. When Annas saw Joseph, he asked, "What are you doing in here?" Joseph answered, "I am with him," meaning Jesus. Annas then asked Jesus about his teachings and about his disciples, Jesus replied: "I have only taught openly where all the Jews come together, in synagogues or at the temple. I have said nothing in secret, so why ask me what I have said? Ask those who heard me.

They will tell you what I have said." One of the soldiers then slapped Jesus across the face, saying, "That is no way to speak to the high priest!" Jesus said to the soldier, "If I have said something wrong, testify as to what is wrong. But if I spoke the truth, why did you strike me?" Then, Annas gave instructions for the soldiers to hold Jesus until the high priest appeared.

Joseph was standing beside Jesus when Caiaphas appeared. Caiaphas was soon joined by some members of the Sanhedrin and other elders and teachers of the law. Joseph already sensed that they were looking for some evidence, false or otherwise, with which to charge Jesus with the crime of sedition, by which they could cause Jesus to be put to death.

When the hearing was opened, Joseph listened quietly as Caiaphas questioned Jesus, waiting for his turn to speak in Jesus' behalf, in the manner he had previously spoken to the entire Sanhedrin. Caiaphas called on witnesses who came forward and testified falsely against Jesus, but nothing they said was sufficient to warrant his arrest. The most serious complaint against Jesus was that he had said, "I am able to destroy the temple of God and rebuild it in three days." Apparently, remembering what Joseph of Arimathea had previously asked of him and the Sanhedrin, "What if he is our promised Messiah, the Son of God?" Caiaphas then said to Jesus, "Tell us if you the Messiah, the Son of God."

"Yes, it is as you say," Jesus replied. "But I say to all of you: In the future you will see the Son of Man sitting at the right hand of the Mighty One and coming on the clouds of heaven."

Then, believing in his heart that the response made by Jesus just could not possibly be true, Caiaphas, endeavoring to demonstrate to all present his own righteous piety, albeit feigned and political, arose and tore his garments, crying at the top of his voice, "Blasphemy! He has spoken blasphemy! You have heard this man speak blasphemy! Now, what do you think?"

Those seated with Caiaphas cried out, as if on some prearranged cue, "He is worthy of death!" The crowd of bystanders, urged on by the accusation, took up the cry, "He has blasphemed! He is worthy of death!" Then, crowding around Jesus, they spit in his face and struck him with their fists. Joseph of Arimathea threw himself around Jesus as best he could to accept many of their blows against his own body.

Momentarily, the soldiers broke up the melee and the hostile crowd pulled back. Some of them, however, continued to hurl terrible, insulting epithets toward Jesus. "Blasphemer!" some yelled. "If you are the Son of God, tell us who struck you," others taunted. Still, others cried out."Where is your power, now?" Jesus had a bruised lip, but he seemed unshaken by the whole affair. Joseph glanced in the direction where Peter had been sitting and saw that Peter was now standing with his back turned, having moved farther away from the fire.

Caiaphas then instructed the soldiers to take Jesus before Pontius Pilate, whose court was at the Praetorium, in Herod's upper palace located in the Upper City of Jerusalem. They wheeled Jesus out of Caiaphas's courtyard to take him to Pilate. Joseph of Arimathea, still close to Jesus, started to go with him, but on a signal from Caiaphas, Joseph's way was blocked at the door and he was compelled to remain inside the courtyard of the high priest.

Not given an opportunity to speak on behalf of Jesus before, Joseph now approached Caiaphas and those members of the Sanhedrin that were there with him. Joseph inquired of Caiaphas, "What have you done? I have always considered you a fair-minded person, thoughtful and just. What has possessed you to do this thing? How could you, when you must know in your heart that Jesus has done no wrong?"

Caiaphas wheeled on Joseph like a man possessed. He flung his words toward Joseph, "He blasphemed! You must have heard with your own ears the words of his own testimony, claiming that he is 'the Christ, the Son of God?'"

Joseph looked squarely into the eyes of Caiaphas and, in a thoughtful tone of voice, asked him, "But what if Jesus really is our long awaited Messiah?"

Caiaphas, laughingly, scoffed, "Him? He cannot possibly be the Messiah for, as the high priest, I would recognize him. When the Messiah comes, God will tell me who he is. This man is only a pathetic pretender, another Zealot who would be king and start trouble for us with Rome. It is better that he should die than all of us."

Caiaphas was adamant about Jesus. He refused to listen any further. He was certain that Jesus was an imposter, a fraud, and there was nothing Joseph of Arimathea could say or do that would budge Caiaphas, or his court cronies, from their mind set against Jesus of Nazareth. Caiaphas' parting words to Joseph were, "Watch your step, sir!" "Watch our step before charges are brought against you!"

Joseph of Arimathea was crushed. The events, as they unfolded that night, seemed like a terrible nightmare. Beginning with Jesus' arrest, everything had been so unscrupulously prearranged beforehand that there simply was no time to mount a defense for Jesus. One event followed another so quickly that it was difficult to keep abreast of the brash trail of contrived, distorted, and ruthless happenings.

Joseph of Arimathea realized that Jesus of Nazareth had challenged the Temple's laws of ritual and diet, but never had he denied or attacked the moral or ethical laws of Israel. In fact, Jesus had always been meticulous in his observance of and obedience to Israel's ancient moral and ethical laws. These laws were carefully handed down from Moses to generation after generation, and Jesus was ever faithful in keeping these ancient codes of Jewish religious faith.

Knowing Jesus as he did all these years, Joseph of Arimathea knew that Jesus would never commit an act, or ever say anything, which would actually warrant his arrest. His teachings were only that the Temple's laws regarding ritual and diet were observances of conscience and situation, rather than being absolute requirements in every instance or occasion.

Even the upsetting of the tables in the Court of the Gentiles, Joseph now realized, was justified, because those tables were a misuse of the Temple court. Those had authorized the misuse of that space had trampled God's directives. Yet, it was Jesus' attitude about the lesser laws of ritual and diet which challenged and angered the temple leaders. Only this, and Caiaphas' accusation about Jesus being a Zealot, was the basis for Jesus being accused and arrested that night.

The more serious charge now, however, was that of blasphemy, Jesus' acknowledgment of himself as the Messiah, the Son of God. Still, given a fair trial, Joseph believed that Jesus could back up that assertion if he were given time and opportunity to do so. He also reasoned that Jesus would never be given such a opportunity by the poison minded Sanhedrin of Caiaphas. He believed that all was not yet hopeless, however, because a charge of blasphemy within the Jewish religion was not, in and of itself, an offense that would warrant a sentence of death before a Roman court.

Having been halted and separated from Jesus, who was now being shuffled before Pilate, Joseph reasoned that Pilate would look into the matter and, finding no justifiable reason to hold Jesus on the petty, trumped up charges made by Caiaphas, Pilate would order Jesus released. He imagined that, following his release, Jesus would then rejoin his disciples on the Mount of Olives, or he could rejoin his mother in The Upper Room.

For Joseph, this had been a terrible night of horrors. He now found himself experiencing shortness of breath, and he was wet with perspiration. Everything around him was crashing down, and he found himself thinking, "If I could only stir myself to wakefulness, perhaps I would discover that I am only having a terrible dream." Yet, sadly, he knew otherwise.

There being nothing further which Joseph of Arimathea could hope to accomplish that night, considering the mood the chief priests had stirred among the gathered crowd, Joseph reasoned, he would wait until morning, after the people's passions had run their course, and then see what he could do. With that hope in mind, Joseph finally was permitted to leave and return to his quarters.

A couple hours of much needed sleep would help revive his exhausted body and bring new strength to his weary mind.

Chapter 9 – A Time of Reflection

Back in his quarters, but unable to sleep, Joseph of Arimathea lay quietly upon his bed. The thoughts and events of the past thirty-three years came flooding into the forefront of his mind. Joseph had recently returned to Palestine from Saluria, England, where he lived much of the year with his family. Those days from Passover to the Festival of Lights, however, had for several years provided Joseph and his family occasion to spend time in Palestine, with opportunity to visit family, attend to business ventures and, for Joseph, at least until now, to serve as a highly respected member of the Sanhedrin Council.

While Joseph was born in Arimathea, located in a remote part of Samaria, not far from the seaport of Joppa, his family was related to the family of Jesus. Joseph's father was Ruben, son of Simon. Ruben was a first cousin of Hannah, the grandmother of Joseph and Mary. Joseph of Arimathea had married Anna, his second cousin, who was the youngest child of Matthan and Hannah. Joseph of Arimathea's own immediate family had for many years resided in Cornwall, England. Still, however, they maintained an annual sojourn to Palestine to visit with relatives and to participate in the yearly feast of Passover, and usually remaining until the Festival of Lights.

In Siluria and Cornwall, and the adjacent area of Wales, Joseph was a successful merchant involved in the tin trade, as well as obtaining lead from Sussex and coal from Wales. After mining and smelting the ores, Joseph shipped the resulting products from the West Coast of England to ports in Europe and throughout the Mediterranean. An astute business person, his trade had made him a very wealthy man.

When they were young, the children of Joseph of Arimathea and Anna, had always enjoyed the annual sojourn to Palestine with their parents, where they would visit their grandparents and family in Palestine. However, they were now occupied with their own lives in Wales and the southwest of England.

His daughter, Penardim, had married Llyr Lediaith. They had a family of their own, now grown. Penardim's son, Bran, named after her much beloved younger brother, lived at Trevan Llanilid, Glamorganshire, Wales. Later, he would become King of Siluria, would become Britain's first royal convert to Christianity, and would become known as "Bran the Blessed Sovereign." Bran would travel to Rome and be baptized by the Apostle Paul. His baptism occurred while Paul was a prisoner there. Bran's son, Caradoc, and his grandsons Cyllinus and Cynon, sons of Caradoc, would be baptized at the same time. Bran would later resign the crown to his son in order to spend his remaining years advancing Christianity throughout England.

Bran, the son of Joseph of Arimathea and Anna, would later become known as Beli, and he was also the King of Siluria. His wife was a delightful young lady, named Gladdys. Their firstborn son was, Amalech. Their second child, a daughter, was named Elena. With pressing business interests and responsibilities for his young family, Bran was unable to accompany his father to Palestine this year.

Joseph of Arimathea had, for the first time, made his yearly pilgrimage to Palestine unaccompanied, his beloved Anna having died during the previous winter. Memories of Anna now filled Joseph's heart with great warmth. He retreated into those memories for a few moments, savoring their sweet comfort. Without thinking, Joseph reached across the bed, needing Anna to be there. When his outstretched hand felt only a cold pillow, Joseph of Arimathea wept deeply.

Anna's father, Matthan, had inherited the official title, King of Israel, in behalf of his wife Hannah, whose descent from King David, through her father Levi, was from a line older than his own. Matthan and Hannah had spent their home life in the quiet town of Nazareth, located in the healthy uplands, about twelve miles from Capernaum. Matthan was a carpenter by trade, engaged in the construction business in the area around the Sea of Galilee. His business was a substantial enterprise and, upon his death, was inherited by his two sons, Heli and Jacob. Matthan and Hannah's oldest daughter, Elizabeth, had married a distant cousin, a priest by the name of Zechariah, and they were the parents of a son named John, known as "the Baptist." Thus, the family's relationship chart looked like this:

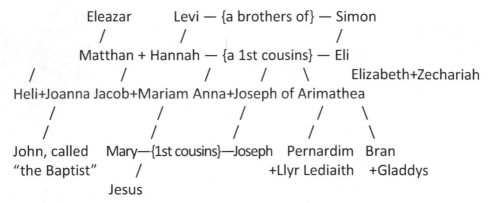

Not shown in the genealogical relationship diagram is a younger daughter of Heli and Joanna, the younger sister of Mary named Salome, who married Zebedee of Capernaum. They were the parents of James and John, first cousins to Jesus, who became his ardent believers, companions, and disciples.

Also not shown are natural children born to Joseph and Mary who are: James born about seven CE, Simeon born about eight CE, Joses born about nine CE, Hannah (Anna) born about ten CE, Mariam born about eleven CE, Jude born about twelve CE, and Claudia born in seventeen CE. (Note: Each of them completely believed in their older half-brother, Jesus, and after his death each one became deeply involved in the formation and rise of the Early Christian Church, along with every single member of their large extended family).

Heli, as the eldest son of Matthan and Hannah, inherited his father's title, King of Israel. Having no son to inherit the title, Heli adopted Joseph, the son of his brother, Jacob. At the same time Joseph was bethothed to wed Heli's daughter, Mary. It was a marvelous way to keep things in the family. Thus, "King of Israel," was a birthright inherited by Jesus of Nazareth, the firstborn son of Mary.

These thoughts about his Anna, their family, and the faded years, now flashed through Joseph of Arimathea's memory as he lay alone, softly sobbing with loneliness in his darkened room on this now stilled night.

Chapter 10 – Thoughts of Yesterday

Joseph of Arimathea's thoughts ran back to the events surrounding Jesus' birth. Joseph and his family were preparing to return to England when Mary and Joseph's first child was born. Being from the town of Arimathea, Joseph had journeyed there to register, according to the mandated registration issued by Augustus Caesar. He had hastened to return to Nazareth that he might also accompany his wife and her family to register in Bethlehem, in Judea, their ancestral home.

Bethlehem was crowded when they arrived and there was no accommodation in either of the three rooming houses in that small, sleepy town. While he and Anna were invited by a close friend to share their home, they had decided to remain with Anna's family who had established some tents for lodging, located near some animal stables. When Mary's birth pains began, the women, his wife Anna, Mary's mother Joanna, and Joseph's mother Mariam, quickly cleaned out one of the stables and made a bed of covered straw on which the young Mary give birth to her firstborn child.

That year, almost immediately after Joseph of Arimathea and his family had arrived in Palestine from Siluria, he had learned from his wife, Anna, the shocking news about Mary's expectant child. Whispers within family circles related Mary's story; how she had became pregnant through a visitation to her by an angel of God. Almost everyone shook their heads in disbelief, yet, likewise, they all found it difficult to disbelieve the account given by Mary. After all, Mary enjoyed a high reputation of impeccable conduct and honesty. They all found it incredulous that Mary would ever do anything which would bring shame or discredit upon herself or her family.

Then, Joseph was able to affirm Mary's account by relating how he, too, had been visited in a dream by an angel who confirmed Mary's story. When Elizabeth and Zechariah arrived and revealed that the long barren Elizabeth was also an expectant mother; relating how her growing baby leaped within her in the presence of Mary, heads quickly turned from questioning to the probability of the impossible. The entire family, of course, was uncertain about what this all meant. Their decided course of action was to keep all this quiet, keep it within the family, and await the outcome to be revealed by God himself in God's own good time.

Shortly thereafter, Joseph of Arimathea sailed with his family back to England. They were unawares of the later visit by the Shepherds and the Magi until they received a dispatch from Anna's family that following winter. Upon their arrival in Palestine again, to celebrate the Passover, they learned that Herod had ordered that all male children in the area of Bethlehem, under the age of two, were to be slain. They also learned that Joseph, being warned in a dream by an angle, and in order to protect their small son, he and Mary had fled, with Jesus, to Egypt.

News had been secreted back in Palestine informing the family of their safe arrival in Egypt, the fact that they were well, and that Joseph had found work. Joseph and Mary would remain in Egypt until after the death of Herod, when Joseph was again informed by an angel, in another dream, that it would be safe for him and Mary to return, with Jesus, to Palestine. Upon their return, they resided in Nazareth, where their parents and grandparents also resided. It was in Nazareth where Jesus grew to manhood.

The family gatherings during those ensuing years always abounded with stories about the children, especially John and Jesus. Although John was a scant four months older than Jesus, John was actually the cousin of both Jesus' mother and father. The children's play time during their family's annual gathering, habitually found John dressing himself up in the make-believe attire of a Rabbi, pretending to read from the Torah, and preaching to Jesus and his other young cousins.

As John's older cousins grew to adulthood, it was Jesus whom John coerced into joining his imaginary temple audience. The family enjoyed telling how Jesus, sitting very still and with a serious bent, would later correct John about his scriptural presentations. Jesus would also ask questions which John was unable to answer, but never did Jesus leave John without a way out; rather, he always encouraged John to fulfill his calling.

Then, of course, there was everyone's favorite story of how Joseph and Mary discovered Jesus missing during a return trip to Nazareth from their visit to the Temple in Jerusalem. Joseph walked ahead with the other men and Mary thought Jesus was with him. Mary walked a good distance behind the men, with the other women, and Joseph assumed that Jesus was walking with her. When Joseph and the men stopped to allow the women to catch up with them, they discovered that Jesus was nowhere to be found. Jesus was twelve years of age at the time.

Hurriedly, they retraced their steps to Jerusalem and to their hearts delight, they discovered their young son still in the Temple. Jesus was discussing profound religious matters with the temple elders. The elders were amazed that such a young boy would know enough to test their skills, sometimes beyond their ability to immediately respond with a sufficient answer. On some religious matters, Jesus was, in fact, teaching the elders. The family loved to relate how Jesus was such an astute scholar.

Joseph of Arimathea then recounted to himself the year that Jesus, an astoundingly bright lad of eighteen years, had accompanied his family back to England. Jesus' father had prevailed upon Mary that such a journey would be an opportunity to afford Jesus an extension to his already keen spiritual and educational insight. Such an experience would greatly broaden Jesus' perspective about the world in which he lived. Jesus would also have the opportunity to see and understand what it took to make the vast business enterprise of his great-uncle's succeed.

Finally, conceding that Joseph of Arimathea would indeed be an excellent mentor to introduce Jesus to the world of business, Mary had agreed that Jesus would go to England. Joseph and his family, with Jesus in tow, sailed from Joppa a week later. It took them thirty-nine days to reach Falmouth, Cornwall, with five ports of call along the way. The end of a late Fall season was almost gone, and Winter was in the air.

Joseph of Arimathea was always amused by the uncanny curiosity shown by Jesus during the six months spent traveling with Joseph and his son, Bran. He was fascinated by the way tin ore was extracted from the pits, sorted, and then processed by smelting. But Jesus seemed more interested in the workmen, themselves, and pleased that they were well paid, respected, and cared for by his great-uncle.

Jesus made friends easily, and accepted more than a few invitations to sup and spend time in the homes of some of the Sularia and Cornwall men and their families. On these occasions, he was always accompanied by Joseph of Arimathea, who was careful in his oversight of Jesus; a promise he had made to his niece, Mary.

Topics of conversation often turned to the subject of religion, and Jesus seemed genuinely interested in their Celtic beliefs. More than once, Jesus would say, "You have your Druid and the Jews have a Rabbi, and while there is great difference in the rituals of worship, we all have the same Father. Do we not all care deeply above the same things in this life as we care about life after this life? Are we, then, not brothers of the same Father, both in this world and in the world to come?"

Joseph of Arimathea remembered that Jesus also once said: "If you knew fully the things which I know, you would no longer honor this world nor the things of this world. The hour is coming when you will know the things of which I speak. Then you will be filled, and you will know my Father."

These men of Sularia and Cornwall really liked Jesus, but they asked Joseph of Arimathea if all people from the other side of the earth talked in that strange, "other seeing," manner? Chuckling to himself, Joseph of Arimathea fell asleep.

Centuries later, William Blake would write a poem to commemorate this visit to England by the young Jesus of Nazareth, in the company of his granduncle, Joseph of Arimathea.

"JERUSALEM'" (from "Milton")
William Blake (1757-1827)

And did those feet in ancient time
Walk upon England's mountains green?
And was the holy Lamb of God
On England's pleasant pastures seen?
And did the Countenance Divine
Shine forth upon our clouded hills?

And was Jerusalem builded here
Among these dark Satanic Mills?
Bring me my bow of burning gold!
Bring me my arrows of desire!
Bring me my spear! O clouds, unfold!
Bring me my chariot of fire!

I will not cease from mental fight,
Nor shall my sword sleep in my hand,
Till we have built Jerusalem
In England's green and pleasant land.

Chapter 11 – Day of the Cross

The banging on the door of his room by a chambermaid caused Joseph of Arimathea to sit bolt upright in his bed. He had slept much later than he intended. Elizar, his servant and companion, was also still asleep. By the time Joseph and Elizar had splashed some water on their faces, dressed, and stumbled down the stairs to the street below, the sun was already high in the sky and he was late. He sent Elizar in search of some food, with instructions to meet him at the address where Nicodemus was staying.

Then, remembering the women who had spent the night in The Upper Room, Joseph retraced his steps back up the stairs only to discover they had already departed the premises. Back down the stairs, the clear skies and sunlit day would make any person glad to be alive. However, there was an important matter to be settled. Joseph went in search of Nicodemus, whom he hoped would support him in his efforts.

Having found Nicodemus, Joseph informed him, as they and their servants walked, about the turn of events during the previous night. As the four of them walked past the house of Caiaphas, also located in the Lower City section of Jerusalem and the place where Jesus had been so ill treated following his arrest the previous night, everything seemed quiet; almost deserted.

They continued on to the Praetorium, Herod's upper palace located in the Upper City section of Jerusalem, where Caiaphas had instructed that Jesus was to be taken before the court of Pontius Pilate. They made inquiry of the guards outside, who told there was no one inside such as they described. Joseph and Nichodemus commented to each other about these facts as they began to appear and they wondered if, after all, everything had been settled with some degree of sanity. With that hope in mind, they turned and walked toward the Temple.

What Joseph of Arimathea and Nicodemus, at this point did not know, but were later to learn, it had not been until shortly after dawn before Caiaphas finally sent Jesus to Pontius Pilate. However, discovering that Jesus was a Galilean, Pilate would shuffle him off to King Herod, who was the ruler in Galilee and who, at that time, was staying at the Hasmonean palace which was also located in the Upper City. But Herod could find no reason to hold Jesus, therefore, he had Jesus returned to Pilate's Court.

Pilate, who by this time had relocated to the Antonio palace which was located adjacent to the Temple, in the Bezetha section of Jerusalem. Pilate had attempted to avoid dealing with those who accused Jesus of such ridiculous charges, but Caiaphas' spies kept him informed of Pilate's new location.

Caiaphas and his ring of Pharisees were, one way or another, determined to be rid of Jesus. Pilate, with no lawful justification to hold Jesus, made several efforts to release him but was afraid to do so because of the insistent clamor of the hostile crowd who thronged his court shouting, "Crucify Him! Crucify Him!" Although Pilate could find no fault in Jesus, fearing a riot, he finally surrendered Jesus into the hands of the chief priests, saying, "Here is your man, you crucify him." Thus, Joseph and Nicodemus would learn that the fate of Jesus was irrevocably sealed.

Jesus would now die by crucifixion; a method of execution the crafty plotters believed would discredit Jesus' standing and credibility among those who followed him. With his impending death, the chief priests would now be rid of this Jesus of Nazareth, whom the crowds now mocked, sarcastically hailing him as, "King of the Jews."

Not knowing the condemnation of Jesus had already taken place, as Joseph of Arimathea, Nicodemus, and their servants walked toward the Temple, they noticed, up a cross street on their left, a crowd of people running, like something important was happening. As if by instinct and without speaking, they moved to follow the crowd as fast as they could possibly move. Fearful dread began to fill Joseph's pumping heart. The throng of gathering people became too great for them to press through, so they turned and took a side street in their effort to try and get ahead of the crowd. Finally they were able to reach the far end of the roadway which led to one of the gates leading out of the city.

That is when they saw Jesus, his face and body badly bruised and bleeding, limping along, barely able to stand, being forced onward by the whips of two soldiers. His walk was more of a stumble and he fell several times, only to be prodded and beaten until he struggled again to his feet and moved forward. Someone had placed on Jesus' head a platted crown made of thorns, which dug deep into his skull. Another man followed nearby, carrying a cross arm that evidently was meant for Jesus. The whole, horrific scene was a picture of agony.

Joseph and Nicodemus finally managed to squeeze through the gate and scamper up the road which ended at Golgotha. It was called by some as "the place of the skull," but to others it was known as a hill called Mount Calvary. They knew what such a journey to that hill meant! Joseph had never before witnessed a crucifixion, but now the Son of God was made to go to that place. The anguish in Joseph's heart was beyond measure.

Reaching the crest of Mount Calvary, where their two servants soon followed and caught up with them, they saw two other men already in the throes of crucifixion. Jesus was being made to lie on his back while his hands were affixed to the crossbar which the other man had been forced to carry.

The soldiers proceeded to secure Jesus' hands to the crossbar, using spike nails for their task. One lick, then two, then three, and a nail were driven through the palm of Jesus' right hand. The same procedure then nailed down his left hand. It was an awful sight. Joseph could feel within himself the pain caused by those nails, with each lick of the hammer, as they were driven through the flesh of Jesus' hands.

The soldiers next tied a rope around each of Jesus' wrists, to prevent the weight of his body tearing the flesh of his hands, thus causing his body to fall forward and cause his premature death. The ropes would help hold his body erect on the cross and prolong the agony of his dying.

Then, the soldiers placed a longer piece of timber under the body of Jesus, perpendicular to the crossbar, and tightly secured the crossbar to it with another rope. At the sole of Jesus' feet they nailed a smaller crossbar, two pieces of wood angled to each other, upon which Jesus could stand, his body being maintained in an upright position.

They also nailed his feet to that angled wood. It was horrendous! Last, they nailed a sign above his head inscribing, in three different languages, the crime for which he was being crucified. The sign read, "This is Jesus, the King of the Jews."

Satisfied with these gruesome preparations for Jesus' crucifixion, the soldiers hoisted the person of Jesus, now fixed onto a T shaped cross, neatly plopping the cross into a hole which had, for that purpose, been previously hewn out of the rocky surface. To prevent the cross from tilting, they braced the cross upright by filling the hole with smaller stones. Finally, the soldiers stood back and, looking up, they smiled in satisfaction as they admired their workmanship.

Jesus was crucified between the two thieves already hanging there, one of either side of him. Joseph felt numb, and sick in his empty stomach.

Mary, the mother of Jesus was there, standing with two of her other sons, James and Joses, along with the other women who had spent the night with her in The Upper Room. Nearby were some of the disciples Jesus had with him in The Upper Room that previous evening. There were obviously many other followers of Jesus around the cross, because there were many people weeping. Many of them were now kneeling. Of course, there was a large contingent of hecklers who hurled shouts of derision: "Save yourself, if you are the son of God!" "Come down from the cross if you are the son of God!" "You saved others, now save yourself if you can!" "You said you could rebuild the Temple in three days, now rescue your own life!" Even one of thieves being executed on one of the crosses beside him, jeered at Jesus. But, those who loved Jesus, continued their solemn watch; they continuously wept, prayed, and held onto each other.

Joseph moved around the encircled crowd to stand beside Jesus' mother, Mary. He, too, would keep the watch. He took her left arm in his left hand, and placed his right arm around her body, as if it was a gesture to lift her up, as well as signaling his deep affection and his great compassion. It was a horrendous scene.

James moved to place his arms around his mother and his great-uncle Joseph, with Joses holding his mother at her right side. The other women closed the circle in front of Mary. Then, one by one, others moved to include themselves in the growing circle, including some of the chosen disciples of Jesus. The remaining disciples stood apart, not knowing exactly what to do, but within the circle there grew a certain power of love they all felt and would always thereafter talk about. There were no shouts of dismay, only weeping and prayers. In the face of death, something amazing was happening among them.

Caiaphas had wanted Pilate to change the sign posted over Jesus' head changed so that it would read instead, "This is Jesus, who says he is King of the Jews," but Pilate refused to change the wording to satisfy Caiaphas' desires. As the wording stood, they served to rebuke Caiaphas for his insistence on crucifying the One who was indeed his king. Pilate may have had the last laugh on Caiaphas, but as he read those words, Joseph knew that God, in his own wise way, was having the final word.

Anguished as he was, Joseph took sweet comfort in that singular turn of events, knowing in his heart that it was, indeed, the Messiah of God whom Caiaphas had crucified. He spoke those words of faith to Mary and James, and those words reverberated as a profound profession of faith around their circle of friends, "Jesus is the Messiah!" Over and over they could hear those words of faith being repeated.

It required six grueling hours for Jesus to die upon the cross. During that time, Jesus spoke several times to those who were there, including words of compassion for those who were putting him to death, praying, "Father, forgive them, for they know not what they do." He spoke words of comfort to his mother. There were also words of concern to John copnserning his mother. When one of the thieves on the cross expressed fear of dying and asked Jesus to have mercy on him, Jesus comforted him with this promise, "Today, you shall be with me in paradise." Even in the throes of death, Jesus was thinking of others. Once, when Jesus asked for water, one of the guards provided him with sponge dipped in wine with a mixture of gall, lifting it to Jesus' mouth on a stalk taken from a hyssop plant, but after tasting it, Jesus refused to receive more of the pain numbing mixture.

Then, about the sixth hour Jesus cried out to his heavenly Father, quoting from the Psalms, "My God, what have you forsaken me?" A few moments later, he said, "It is finished Father, into your hands I commend my spirit." With those words, Jesus bowed his head and died. At that time, and until the ninth hour, a strange darkness fell over all the land. Some of those who had taunted Jesus changed their song, and the squad of soldiers standing nearby, including those who had gambled for his robe, also began to grieve. They expressed wonderment why Jesus had to die? The entire eerie scene, from beginning to end, was like a story told around a campfire. It all seemed so unreal. Jesus was dead!

Chapter 12 – Deed of Honor

It was getting late, and darkness was upon the land. Since the Day of Preparation being at hand for the next day's special Sabbath, and with the two men who were crucified with Jesus being still alive on their crosses, some Jewish officials asked Pilate to have their legs broken in order to hasten their deaths. The Jews wanted their bodies removed before the Sabbath began.

Therefore, on orders from Pilate, the soldiers broke the legs of the first man who had been crucified, and then the legs of the other man. But when they came to Jesus, the guards saw that he was already dead so they did not break his legs. Instead, one of the soldiers pierced Jesus' side with a spear, causing a sudden rush of blood and water to flow from his side.

Leaving Nicodemus to remain with the family and disciples of Jesus, Joseph of Arimathea, because he knew what Caiaphas might do to pursue the threats made against him, went to Pilate and asked him for permission to remove and bury the body of Jesus. Pilate gave him signed permission to do so. Returning to Mount Calvary, Joseph persuaded James to escort his mother and the others to The Upper Room, while he and Nicodemus prepared and buried the body of Jesus. This, James agreed to do. Joseph promised that he and Nicodemus would join them later in The Upper Room.

While death is an affair of the entire Jewish community, for Jesus, under the circumstances, there was only Joseph of Arimathea, a fellow member of the Council named Nichodemus, to whom Jesus had said "Ye must be born again," and their two servants. Having received written permission from Pontus Pilate to retrieve the body of Jesus from his place of crucifixion, they transported the body of Jesus to a garden where there was a private tomb previously purchased by Joseph of Arimathea.

Joseph of Arimathea had long ago arranged to have the tomb cut into the rock as a place in which he and Anna would be entombed together when the time came. When Anna had died during the previous winter, however, his children had persuaded him to inter her body in Siluria instead of taking her to Jerusalem. The garden grave in Jerusalem was a "shelf grave," consisting of two benches cut in the vertical face of a large outcropping of rock, upon which two corpses could be placed, as companions, within the tomb. The opening into the grave was made to be closed by a stone slab positioned so it might be rolled into place.

There, outside the tomb, they removed the crown of thorns from Jesus' head and quietly prepared the body of Jesus for burial. They began the process by ritualistic washing and purifying the body. Having sent Elizar to retrieve from his room the silver chalice used by Jesus during the previous night, Joseph caught some blood from Jesus' side into the silver chalice, which Joseph would take to his quarters when they returned there, along with the thorns taken from the head of Jesus. Following this, they dressed the body of Jesus in a white linen shroud, which Elizar had also been instructed to obtain when he went for the silver chalice.

The preparation also included a recitation of prayers from the Psalms, bearing witness to God's promises of triumph in the face of death. When the preparation was finished, they laid the body of Jesus upon one of the rock benches hewn out inside the tomb. Then, Joseph of Arimathea devotedly took his own tallith, or prayer shawl, tied with its four sets of knotted fringes to symbolize the commandment incumbent upon every Jew, and placed it on the body of Jesus. Before placing the prayer shawl on Jesus' body, he cut one of the sets of fringes to show that the person of Jesus was no longer bound by the religious obligations of the living.

Then, with the assistance of their two servants, Joseph of Arimatha and Nicodemus rolled the stone into place and sealed the tomb in which they had placed the body of Jesus of Nazareth. While it was the custom to inscribe the name of the person interred upon the stone slab sealing the grave, darkness was now upon them, and two soldiers had arrived, sent there from Pontius Pilate, to guard the tomb. The task of placing an inscription upon the stone slab would have to wait until after the Sabbath was ended.

In the darkness and gloom of those awful last hours of Jesus, when his disciples having all forsaken him, Judas having sold him for 30 pieces of silver, the chief disciple Peter having denied him with a curse, swearing that he never knew Jesus, the chief priests having found him guilty of blasphemy, and the council having condemned him to death, Joseph went right against the powers that were, and against the advice of his friends he begged Pilate for the body of Jesus and with the help of Nicodemus and their two servants, Joseph of Arimathea had buried the body of Jesus in full accordance with Jewish customs, adding therewith his own love and fervent blessings.

Some might say that Joseph's deed of honor was that of an honorable man caring for his beloved grandnephew, but Joseph knew this was much more – his action was that of a Believer who was laying the earthly body of his Lord to rest in a grave, where he would await his heavenly Father's promise to raise him up in glory to live again. Joseph of Arimathea believed Jesus!

Chapter 13 – Imprisonment

Having completed the task of burying the body of Jesus, Joseph of Arimathea and Nicodemus thought that, to avoid a confrontation with Caiaphas or other members of the Sanhedrin, it would be wise if each of them reentered the city from Mount Calvary by a different route. Nicodemus suggested that Joseph and Elizar return by a nearer route while he and his servant would choose a longer route. That agreed upon, they parted company and each began their return to their quarters in the Lower City section of Jerusalem.

As soon as Joseph and Elizar entered into the streets of Jerusalem, they were accosted by Caiaphas' guards and, while Joseph was compelled to go with them, Elizar was permitted to go free. Joseph provided him with instructions to inform James and the others of his detention. At the same time he entrusted Elizar with the crown of thorns which he had removed from Jesus's head and silver chalice into which he had acquired some of the blood from Jesus' body, telling Elizar to guard with his life the chalice and its contents, along with the crown of thorns. Joseph was then escorted to where Caiaphas and some other members of the Sanhedrin were waiting. One of his many spies had informed Caiaphas that it was Joseph had made inquiry about the body of Jesus, and it was Joseph who had received permission from Pontius Pilate to take and bury the body of Jesus.

When Joseph informed them where he had buried the body of Jesus, Caiaphas immediately dispatched two members of the

Sanhedrin to Pilate to request that guards be sent to guard Jesus' tomb, with the excuse that the followers of Jesus might steal his body and hide it. Actually, when Caiaphas' spy made inquiry about the body of Jesus and this information reported to him, Pilate had himself suspected that Caiaphas might attempt to steal Jesus' body, therefore, Pilate had already ordered that two guards be posted day and night around Jesus' tomb to ensure that it was not disturbed.

In the meantime, while Caiaphas was waiting for a response from Pilate about the guards, he and the remaining members of the Sanhedrin questioned Joseph about his burial of Jesus' body. When Joseph informed them that he had taken and buried the body of Jesus according to the Jewish custom and ritual, Caiaphas and the others became immediately enraged. They railed at Joseph, hurling every imaginable insult and threat upon him, but Joseph remained calm throughout the whole ordeal. If fact, he would say later, "he took great pleasure in their wrathful displeasure, because he knew something in his heart they did not, and probably would never know.

When word was received from Pilate that guards had been posted at the tomb of Jesus, the Sabbath was already full upon them. Deciding to hold Joseph of Arimathea for trial, that event would have to wait until the Sabbath was ended. Thus, they locked Joseph in a windowless room, placed guards outside the single entry into the room, and placed the seal of Caiaphas upon the door's lock to ensure Joseph's undisturbed confinement, deferring their plan to return when the Sabbath was over and deal with Joseph at that time for having buried the body of Jesus according to Jewish custom and ritual.

Joseph had eaten only a small bite that morning, brought to him by his servant Elizar while Joseph was seeking Nicodemus. Joseph was hungry, but he reasoned that he would have to endure without food for at least another twenty-four hours. But, with a satisfied smile within himself, he knew he could endure. Contented, Joseph made a small pallet for himself and went to sleep in his place of confinement.

Joseph slept quite well that night, not waking until long after he thought morning must have come. He could not tell for sure because his room was totally dark, except for a small glimmer of light which shone under the locked and sealed door into his place of confinement. Without light, food, or any single thing to amuse him or to occupy his time, Joseph spent a lot of time in prayer. After all, this was the Passover Sabbath. He also spent a great deal of time remembering those things of which had heard Jesus speak. And, of course, what Jesus had said to him about being the Son of God, the Messiah. Joseph did not know what the future held for Christ, or for himself, but there was within Joseph a certain assurance that all this, somehow, was only the beginning.

After what seemed an eternity of hours, the glimmer of light under the door to Joseph's place of confinement grew almost black, causing Joseph to reason that night had fallen again and the Sabbath had ended. When, after the longest of time, Caiaphas and his friends had not returned for him, Joseph reasoned they had decided to wait until morning to come for him. After all, Joseph was in a secured room, locked and sealed. Joseph was not going anywhere. Joseph felt the pangs of hunger. He had carried on himself a small flask of water, but this was now empty. If it was a waiting game Caiaphas was playing, they had the deck of cards but Joseph believed in a strange and powerful way that it was he who held the trump cards. As things were, Joseph went to sleep, satisfied.

Surviving documents show that the Sanhedrin confronted Joseph of Arimathea that night for his actions of having buried Jesus. Then they arrested him when Joseph accused them of killing the Messiah and renounced them for their unrepentant behavior. They placed Joseph in a cell, placed a seal upon the cell door, but when they returned Joseph was gone – yet the seal was unbroken.

Chapter 14 – Miraculous Delivery

Joseph of Arimathea left a journal, which still survives. In it he wrote, "While I was sleeping, someone appeared in my cell, washing me with water, bathing me with ointment, all the time kissing me, and I smelled the sweet perfume he was pouring over my head. When I was told to open my eyes, I saw the risen Christ. With him was Demas, the saved robber who was crucified with Jesus. I learned also that the name of the unrepentant robber was Gestas. Jesus expressed to me his profound gratitude for my having so tenderly buried his earthly body. Jesus then released me from my prison cell, lifting me from the cell by the four corners of the cloth on which I had lain, and took me home to Arimathea, telling me to remain there until I was sent for."

Joseph of Arimathea, having been taken to by Jesus from Jerusalem to his home in Arimathea , awaited there in his manor house according to the instructions given to him, until he was sent for. When he came downstairs the next morning, everyone was filled with joy to see him, but they were surprised at the same time because they did not know how he had gotten into the carefully locked house, or even upstairs to his bedroom quarters without being seen. His reply to their questions about this was, "Oh, I managed." The smiling twinkle in his eye made them think that Joseph must have some secret entrance into the house which no one else knew about.

Joseph came downstairs as his brother Ely, his wife Orpah, and their family, were preparing to partake of their morning meal. Joseph was hungry and a fabulous breakfast was quickly set before him by the servants. As they dined, Joseph related for them the events which had occurred in Jerusalem, informing them of Jesus' crucifixion and the antagonism demonstrated by Caiaphas and other members of the Sanhedrin. He also told them of invaluable assistance given to him by Nicodemus and the support they had received from Gamaliel and Simon.

Suddenly, remembering that he had sent James, Joses, and their mother Mary and the others to The Upper Room, promising to soon join them there, he told them about his being accosted by Caiaphas and his allies, about his imprisonment, and how he had sent his servant Elizar to let them know where he was. Now, however, Elizar and the others did not know where Joseph was. Joseph asked Ely if one of this trusted servants could be sent to Jerusalem to bring Elizar home to Arimathea, and also to inform James, Joses, and their mother Mary, that Joseph was safe in Arimathea. Ely went immediately to attend to the matter, returning shortly with a servant named Mashon. Joseph provided him with written directions, including the message that those in The Upper Room could continue to use it if they so desire. Mashon was immediately dispatched to carry out his duties in Jerusalem and to return with Elizar to Arimathea.

When Mashon had departed, Ely asked many questions of Joseph, wanting especially to know about his burial of Jesus' body and his subsequent arrest. Joseph told him everything as it happened, except he said nothing concerning his miraculous escape or how he arrived home in Arimathea.

When Ely asked how he managed to escape, Joseph would only wink with a smile and say, "I managed." Joseph was not yet ready to reveal to anyone, not even his brother, that the risen Christ had miraculously freed him from his place of confinement, then carried him home to Arimathea by the four corners of a cloak.

Who could possibly believe such a story? Things like that just do not happen in the usual course of events. Joseph would reveal his having seen the Risen Christ and the means of his rescue at a later time, but for now he kept it to himself lest others think him touched in the head.

Back in Jerusalem, Caiaphas and members of the Sanhedrin were wondering how Joseph had managed to escape from his place of confinement. The door to the room where Joseph had been compelled to stay was still locked and the seal of Caiaphas remained unbroken or tampered with when they arrived to get Joseph on the morning after the Passover Sabbath.

Caiaphas himself had examined, broken his seal, and unlocked the door. Finding the room empty and Joseph gone, they had questioned the guards who, to a man, reported nothing unusual had happened in their presence. Every inch of the room was then inspected, but they found nothing to indicate how Joseph might have escaped his captivity. It was a complete mystery to Caiaphas and the others.

By the following day, Caiaphas' and the others began to hear the strange news that was being repeated in the streets. " Jesus was alive!" the stories told. Jerusalem was abuzz with the message that, "Jesus was risen from the dead!" "The stone is rolled away and the tomb is empty," another report said. Caiaphas received yet another report from one of his spies that, "One the first day of the week, Jesus had appeared to some women who had gone early to his tomb.

Caiaphas had his spies working everywhere in an effort to locate the body of Jesus, certain that someone must have stolen his body and hid it. Nowhere, however, could his spies find the body of Jesus nor could they locate anyone who might know anything about such a thing. Now, to make matters worse for Caiaphas, people throughout Jerusalem were referring to Jesus as the "Christ," saying, "Christ is Risen!"

Caiaphas was beside himself! His anger raged! "First, someone steals and hides the body of that Galilean, and now they are calling him the Christ," he said to his fellow Sanhedrin members. Then comes a report that two men, walking to Emmaus on the evening of the first day, had been visited by the risen Jesus, and they recognized him as he supped with them. Next news comes to us that the risen Jesus has appeared somewhere here in Jerusalem to a group of his followers. Now, this has been followed by more information, claiming that two men traveling from Galilee to Jerusalem Jesus upon a mountain, meeting with his disciples.

It seemed to Caiaphas that stories about Jesus were popping up everywhere, and he was determined to put an end to them all. But when he put his foot down to squelch the Lord in one place, Christ would pop up somewhere else, always ahead of the best efforts put forth by Caiaphas.

Caiaphas was a highly intelligent man. He had not been chosen the high priest without some astuteness and ability. In this case, Caiaphas decided to take a different approach in the matter of Jesus. He pretended to embrace the Christ, sending his spies in search of persons reported to have seen the Risen Lord, telling them that Caiaphas would like to see them because he wished to gather and proclaim any and all of the wonderful news concerning Christ. It was a clever trap by which to capture those who followed Jesus.

His spies, however, were unable to locate any of the disciples because they were in hiding. It was then reported that the two men from Galilee had left Jerusalem and returned home. Someone offered the possibility that the disciples of Jesus were likewise in Galilee because most of them were Galileans. Still, others claimed they had reason to believe the disciples were somewhere in Samaria.

Caiaphas decided that he would send his spies, and other servants as well, to make a search throughout the land in an effort to locate anyone who had seen Jesus or who had in any way ever been connected with him. They went accordingly, returning as soon as possible to report to Caiaphas they had not been successful in their search to locate any of the disciples of Jesus, nor the two men from Emmaus, nor the two men from Galilee, but two men did return and inform Caiaphas that they had learned that Joseph of Arimathea had been located at his home in Samaria. Caiaphas had almost forgotten about Joseph and his escape from confinement. Samaria was outside the Sanhedrin's jurisdictional authority. It would be necessary to entice Joseph of Arimathea to come to Jerusalem.

While all of this activity was going on in Jerusalem, in Arimathea and Samaria everything seemed at the moment to be the same as usual. Elizar had returned to Arimathea. He had brought Joseph the silver chalice containing the blood of Christ, which Joseph had provided for Jesus to use at his last supper with his disciples. The silver chalice and the silver tray were inside a special crafted olive wood lined case which came with them at the time of their purchase.

Elizar had also brought the good news about the women, those who went to the tomb of Jesus early on that morning of the first day of the week and had seen the Risen Christ. Then, too, two men walking from Jerusalem to Emmaus that same evening had returned to Jerusalem with the news that they, too, had seen the Risen Christ. "Then," Elizar said, looking toward Joseph, "Christ appeared before his disciples who were gathered in The Upper Room you provided for them to use." "Sire," Elizar said, "Jesus is alive!"

It was then that Joseph explained to his family, to Elizar and the other servants gathered there, the means by which he escaped from his place of confinement in Jerusalem, along with how he had managed to get into his locked house at Arimathea without anybody seeing him arrive or go to his upstairs room.

"I know that it seems like a fairytale, but the fact remains that I have seen the Risen Christ with my own eyes. I saw his face, his hands caressed me, his lips kissed me, and he brought me safely home. O my dear ones, our Savor and Lord has come!"

Everyone present in the room was weeping with unrestrained joy. They embraced each other. Master and servant were one. They prayed, and gave thanks, for Christ the Savior had come! As one, they exclaimed, "Thanks be to God!"

Chapter 15 – ATTEMPTED RECONCILIATION

When the Sanhedrin learned where Joseph of Arimathea was located, they carefully composed and sent him a message expressing their apology and sorrow at their behavior toward him, explaining that it was the pressure they were under at the time, and asking him to return to Jerusalem and meet with them.

Joseph immediately went to meet with them in Jerusalem, his hopes high with thoughts of reconciliation because, as Caiaphas and the members of the Sanhedrin who signed the letter stated, they now realized they were wrong to misjudge Jesus. Now that Jesus was risen from the dead they, too, desired to proclaim him as God's Messiah.

Joseph of Arimathea's heart was full of joy as he read the Sanhedrin's letter of apology and their acknowledgment of Jesus as God's Messiah. They did not explain in their letter how they had arrived at such a decision, but he was glad they had. The Sanhedrin, on which it had been such a high privilege for Joseph of Arimathea to serve, was prepared to let bygones be bygones if only Joseph would forgive them. He did forgive them! He forgave them because that is what Christ would do! Forgiving them, Joseph was prepared to join with them in reconciliation and he immediately returned to Jerusalem, accompanied by the Sanhedrin's messenger.

Meeting with other members of the Sanhedrin, Joseph told them his story. "While I was sleeping, someone appeared in my cell, washing me with water, bathing me with ointment, all the time kissing me, and I smelled the sweet perfume he was pouring over my head. When I was told to open my eyes, I saw the risen Christ. With him was Demas, the forgiven robber who was crucified with Jesus."

Continuing, Joseph said, "I also learned that the name of the unrepentant robber was Gestas. Jesus expressed his profound gratitude to me for having so tenderly buried his earthly body. Jesus then released me from my prison cell. He lifted the sheet on which I lay by its four corners, carried me out of my place of confinement and took me to my home in Arimathea, telling me to remain there until I was sent for."

As Joseph spoke, he could see the faces of Caiaphas and other members of the Sanhedrin growing redder and more exasperated by the minute. After he had finished speaking, a greatly agitated Caiaphas, and those Sanhedrin members present, began railing at Joseph. Their combined voices became a jumble of nonsense. Old and unrepentant attitudes spilled across their angry lips to again challenge and verbally demean Joseph.

"They have deceived me," Joseph thought. "They are not at all repentant of their loathsome behavior toward me. They have lied to me. They do not believe Christ is risen. Their letter was merely a means of luring me into their contemptible snare. They only want to know how I managed to escape from my former place of confinement without breaking Caiaphas' seal. Well, I told them, but they still do not believe me."

Before they could go any further, perhaps harm him or make him again their prisoner, Joseph wheeled around and, bolting for the door, quickly made his way past Caiaphas' guards standing outside, rushed down the hallway to a door leading to a small courtyard, crossed it, and by another door emerged into a side street. By those movements Joseph managed to slip away from them.

"Well-meaning people, and especially those with power, can be terribly wrong when they are spiritually short-sighted," Joseph thought. "Caiaphas and those others on the Sanhedrin may occupy an exalted position, but they have lost their spiritual balance."

Moving farther away from the Temple, Joseph took a circumventing route in order to reach The Upper Room. He knew that Caiaphas employed a ring of spies who watched everything, and he did not want them to follow him or locate the site of The Upper Room, where James and Mary his mother, and the other followers of Jesus might still be staying.

Down the street from where his quarters and The Upper Room were located, Joseph waited for an hour to see if anyone had followed him. After that time, deciding it was safe to go to his quarters, he first went to his room and remained for a long time, waiting and watching, before finally deciding it was safe to go upstairs to The Upper Room. There he found Mary and the other women, and some of the disciples of Jesus. James and Joses, the brothers of Jesus, were not present, having returned to their own places of residence. However, they informed Joseph, James and Joses both came daily to The Upper Room to share together the good news, to pray and sing hymns, and to discuss what had happened and was happening, as well as discussing ways in which they should now proceed since Christ was risen from the dead and appearing among them with greater frequency.

Joseph related to them how Christ had also appeared to him, rescued him from his place of confinement, and delivered him safely to his home in Arimathea. He also informed them of his encounter that day with Caiaphas and the Sanhedrin, relating how they had written him a letter of apologies in which they pretended to believe in Christ and his resurrection from the grave, but it was only an attempt to lure him into a trap. Joseph told them that Caiaphas and the others were dangerous people and they should be avoided in every possible way.

Joseph also informed them that The Upper Room in which they were now staying had been reserved for three months, and that it and his quarters on the floor below had been previously paid for. He informed them they were welcome to utilize these facilities, and if Caiaphas' spies had not detected their location, he would make arrangements to renew the lease of The Upper Room for as long as it was needed, providing it continued to be a safe place to for them to meet. Joseph explained that the owner of the property was a friend who would keep their meeting place a secret, protecting them as best he could but, individually, they had to be most careful when entering and leaving The Upper Room, in order to keep its location a secret from the spies of Caiaphas.

Joseph explained to everyone present his own thoughts concerning the events of the past few days, telling them, "An unyielding faith in Christ is your most important asset, and no matter what happens, or how disastrous things may seem to be at times, your faith in Christ must never cease because the risen Christ is doing a new thing."

"Like you," Joseph added, "I do not know what this new thing is, but I believe that Christ will make it right and will reveal it at the proper time. This you must also believe," he stressed. "After all," he said, "His Father and our Father has raised him from the dead. And, I know that he was dead because I prepared and buried his body. His resurrection now proves to us the wonderful love and providence of our almighty God."

"In this life, Jesus did many miracles," Joseph continued, "As God's Christ, his power now has no limit except that which he may place upon himself, and whatever Christ does, or whatever happens in the future, it will be for the glory of Christ and his Father and, in turn, it will become their blessing to us."

"Remember this, and keep that faith," Joseph said, "And in his appearances to us, he will surely provide for us the directives which will guide us, from this time and forevermore." Those present exclaimed, as if they spoke with a single voice, "Amen! Amen! Thanks be to God! Amen!"

Joseph then informed them that he was returning to Arimathea. "However, if trouble should come to any of you," he promised, "You will find a safe haven at my home in Arimathea. My home will always be open to receive you, because from this day we are one; one with Christ and one with each other; a family bound together through the Christ we love more than we love our own lives."

With that, Joseph affectionately kissed each person present, they shared a prayer together and, after speaking to the owner and gaining assurance from his friend that he would protect those in The Upper Room, Joseph quietly departed Jerusalem for his home in Arimathea.

Chapter 16 – A Different Path Taken

After Joseph's return his home in Arimathea, he spent a week waiting and wondering what next should be done. He enjoyed the opportunity of again be in the company of his own brother and his family and he took time to renew the fond relationships he had long shared with those who were employed on his estate. Many of them had been with Joseph and his brother for several years.

On one occasion, Joseph went into the village to spend a day visiting with Hezron ben Zerah, a man who had so ably assisted Joseph's father, Eli ben Judah, when he was alive. Hezron, now in his eighty-fourth year, lived with his daughter, and spent his days mostly sitting in the shade of an old olive tree outside the house in which they lived. In his younger days, he had been his father's right hand in overseeing the operations of Arimathean estate.

When Joseph turned the corner and was walking down the road to where Hezron lived with his daughter, ben Zerah immediately recognized him by the peculiar gait with which Joseph had walked since he was a small boy. He adored Hezron, and as a young boy he had loved to follow Hezron around the estate. Joseph still held Hezron ben Zerah in great affection. In the course of their conversation, Joseph told Hezron of the events which had unfolded in Jerusalem, informing him that the Christ had come.

After listening to Joseph tell about all these wonderful events, Hezron ben Zerah praised God for having lived to see the day of

Christ's coming. Sensing Joseph's uncertainty about what to do next, Hezron's advice, as one who had lived for this day, was to be patient until the will of Almighty God and his Christ revealed the way to them. It was the same kind of advice Joseph had given to those in The Upper Room, and Hezron ben Zerah's confirmation pleased Joseph very much.

Thus Joseph of Arimathea began living in two worlds, one being the new age which Christ was bringing into being, and the other was that old world in which he must continue to live his life until the new age came to fruition. One was spiritual, the other was physical. One was with his heart, the other with his body. The first was what he longed for, but the second was of necessity. Joseph still lived in the old world and, until the new had arrived in its full splendor, there remained much to do. "That of the old which remained to be done," Joseph reasoned, "Would make all the difference when the new was fulfilled." Everything else he would leave to the wisdom and glory of God and to his Christ.

Joseph received news from Jerusalem which reported that Christ had appeared again to the disciples in The Upper Room. The report said that Christ came specifically to see Thomas, one of "The Twelve," as they were now calling themselves even though there were only eleven of them remaining. Judas Iscariot had hanged himself because he had betrayed Jesus by arranging for Jesus' arrest in the garden called Gethsamane. Thomas had not been present when Jesus initially visited "The Twelve," and Thomas refused to believe their story about Christ's appearing to the others. When Christ made his appearance a second time, with Thomas being present, Thomas believed."The Twelve" had left Jerusalem immediately afterwards and were traveling to Galilee where Christ had said they would again see him again.

Joseph of Arimathea decided that he, too, was going to Galilee. He also hoped to see again the risen Christ when he appeared there to "The Twelve." "Besides," Joseph told his brother, "I want to visit our relatives in Nazareth and Capernaum." Again, Joseph asked Elizar to go with him as a traveling companion.

In Nazareth, Joseph visited and stayed in the home of his brother-in-law Heli, the father of Mary and grandfather of Mary's son, Jesus. Heli was fifteen years Joseph's senior in age, and the first thing Joseph noticed was how Heli had aged since they last saw each other. This once jovial, intrepid, and extremely kind man, whose hair was now thin and graying, appeared stooped and tired. Heli and his wife Joanna greeted Joseph in a manner which evidenced their great joy in Joseph's presence, but something was missing from the spring in Heli's step and the firmness of his hand. However, while his speech was slower than Joseph remembered, Heli's wit remained as quick as ever.

They were greatly grieved by the news of their grandson's death and they remained in mourning. Heli had lost his brother Jacob, then his older sister Elizabeth and her husband Zechariah, then his brother's son Joseph, followed by his sister Anna's death and, now, the younger generation was being lost; first his nephew John, and now his grandson Jesus. Those losses were hard to bear. Joseph realized that it was more than age which has taken its toll on Heli; the loss of his loved ones, especially the death of Jesus, had clearly magnified the burden in Heli's soul.

Joseph shared with them all the news he had, telling them that Mary and her two sons, James and Joses, were safe. Although they had been witnesses to the crucifixion of Jesus, Joseph said, they had borne their burden and their grief amazingly well. Joseph explained how he and Necodemus had buried the body of Jesus. News had reached Heli and Joanna that their grandson had risen from the grave and was alive, but they considered those stories out of the ordinary; that perhaps someone was using that as a scheme for one thing or another, or even a cruel hoax perpetrated by a twisted mind. Joseph set their hearts at ease when he told them about his own miraculous escape made possible by the risen Christ.

Joseph told them that, he, having buried the body of Jesus, and then having seen Jesus alive afterwards, the resurrection stories they had heard were absolutely true. Both Heli and Anna had many questions to ask concerning the resurrection of Jesus but Joseph, unable to explain how their grandson's resurrection had been possible, could only affirm, "I have seen Jesus alive, and all I know is that I believe it because I know it is true."

"I know he is God's Messiah, the Christ, and I do not have to understand what I know to be true. I can only believe and give God the glory," Joseph added.

Heli then sent messages to their daughter Salome, the wife of Zebedee, and to his brother Jacob's widow, Mariam, and to two of Jesus' sisters, Hanna, Claudia, and their families, informing them that Joseph was visiting in their home, inviting them to come as soon as possible and to share the evening meal with them. All those invited lived in Nazareth. Salome's husband, Zebedee, was in Capernaum where he continued to operate his fishing business. Zebedee was short handed since his two sons, James and John, who had left their father to become disciples of Jesus and members of The Twelve. Joseph told Heli and Joanna that he was going to Capernaum later and would visit those who lived in Capernaum when he went there.

Joseph and Heli spent the remainder of the afternoon in conversation. Joanna was busy overseeing the preparation of the evening meal, but she kept sticking her head in the door every few minutes thinking she might hear additional news about her grandson's resurrection from the dead. Joseph had told them a story that was too good to be true, but if Joseph said it was the truth that was good enough for her; as it was for Heli, who now appeared to be sitting a little straighter and taller.

When those invited had assembled in Heli and Joanna's home to share the evening meal together, as they were eating Joseph told them about his beloved Anna's last days on earth. He had brought a personal message from Anna for each one present, which Anna had made Joseph promise that he would deliver in person.

Each message was neatly folded, addressed, and sealed. Joseph passed them out and they each broke the seal and unfolded the message to read it. In each letter, they discovered, Anna had something wonderful to say about them, offered advice for each to pursue, requested that each do something for her in regard to another member of the family, and then, closed each letter with a curious statement, "When the Christ reveals himself, believe in him with all your heart, for he is your eternal hope and the hope of the world for tomorrow. There will be no peace for any until Christ is the Lord of all."

As each person began sharing their particulars with the others, they discovered each message was entirely different, except for that one, singular, concluding directive from Anna. Joanna read her message second, and as she read those concluding words, everyone's interest turned to them. "Mine says the same thing," Claudia, exclaimed. "So does mine,"said Salome. "Mine, too," said Joanna.

"O my God," said Joseph. "Anna!" As if he were speaking to Anna, Joseph asked, "How could you have known about the coming of Christ? Is this a coincidence, or did you have a premonition?"

It was Joanna who answered him. "Joseph, I am certain that Anna had a vision, because the last time she was here, she told me that she had a dream about the coming of Christ. I never told anyone before now, because Anna asked me to wait until the time was right before I said anything about her dream."

Joseph was stunned beyond further words. Anna had not told him, but there were a lot of things she did not tell him in regard to the birth and the person of Jesus. Joseph knew his Anna carried many holy things in her heart, but the depth of their extent he had never realized.

Heli lifted his arms to heaven, saying, "Anna, you knew! You always knew! You and Elizabeth, Mary and Joseph, too! At last, I understand, I believe, "he cried out, as tears rolled down his cheeks.

They were still praying and singing when James and John, the sons of Salome and Zebedee came into the house. They had only returned from Jerusalem, just now, with "The Twelve" disciples of Jesus. The others were going on to Capernaum, but James and John wanted to stop by their home in Nazareth to let their parents know they were well and safe, as well as sharing with the parents and others in the community the wonderful news about the resurrection of Jesus. They were going on to the shore of Galilee where Jesus had said he would meet them. Joseph then handed James and John their own sealed letters from Anna. After they had opened and read the letters, which contained the same concluding directive, a prayer meeting started all over again.

Joseph of Arimathea announced to them that he had decided to have nothing further to do with Caiaphas and the Sanhedrin. He told them that it was evident to him that he and the Sanhedrin were on different paths. The others' whole heartedly agreed with Joseph, knowing in their hearts the path they would now follow was as followers of Christ, whom they now loved and regarded more highly than their own lives. As much as they cherished the Temple and their Hebrew faith, the House of David would now follow the Christ.

They cited for their example Father Abraham and Sarah, who had left behind the old ways of their people because they dared to obey the Lord and go into a new land. So, henceforth, the House of David would also obey the Lord and move in a new direction, one which the Sanhedrin and the rest of the Jews denied and diametrically opposed. The path they were taking was as clear to those gathered in the home of Heli and Joanna, as light is distinguished from darkness.

The following day, Joseph of Arimathea, accompanying James and John, their mother Salome, their grandparent's, Heli and Joanna, along with Hanna and Claudia, went to Capernaum to meet up with "The Twelve," there to await the promised appearing of Jesus. They were excited, and they earnestly desired to see Jesus.

Chapter 17 – A Higher Calling

Joseph of Arimathea was not present when, in Galilee, the risen Christ appeared again to his disciples. Joseph was absent, visiting and sharing with family members in Capernaum, where he had spent the night, when Christ appeared to the disciples at dawn the following morning. He relished, however, the story as they afterwards related it to him.

The disciples of Jesus had awaited Christ for three days without his appearing to them. Since the catch of fish had of late been short of the supply needed, Peter and Andrew, along with James and John, decided one evening that they would help their family businesses by going fishing. Since they had other disciples as extra help, they cast their boat into the lake hoping to make a banner catch of fish that night.

However, they fished all night and they caught nothing. Early in the morning, as they neared the shore, they encountered a man standing on the shore who asked them if they had any fish. They supposed him to be a potential customer who had came to the lake early, hoping to buy some fish. They told the man they had fished all night without catching any fish. The man called out again, telling them to cast their net on the right side of the boat and they would catch some fish. When they did as the man asked of them, their net was so full they were unable to haul the heavy catch of fish into the boat.

In that moment, John suddenly realized that the man who had spoken to them was Christ, and he said to Peter, "It is the Lord!" Peter immediately put on his outer garment and jumped into the water, making his way toward the shore where Christ stood. The others followed in the boat, dragging the net full of fish with them. When they had landed, they saw that Christ had of fire of burning coals there with fish on it, and some bread. Christ said to them, "bring some fish you have just caught." Peter again climbed aboard the boat and helped the others finish hauling the fish to shore. They were surprised the net had not broke under such a large load of big fish. The risen Christ then extended his arms, as if drawing a circle, and invited them to come and have breakfast.

After they had eaten the breakfast of fish and bread, Christ talked with them, asking Peter, "Simon son of John, do you love me more than these?" "Yes, Lord," Peter answered, "You know that I love you," Jesus said, "Feed my lambs." A few moments later, Christ asked Peter again, "Simon son of John, to you truly love me?" Peter answered again, "Yes, Lord, you know that I love you." Christ said, "Take care of my sheep." For a third time Christ said to Peter, "Simon son of John, do you love me?" Peter replied, "Lord, you know all things; you know that I love you." Christ said to him for a third time, "Feed my sheep."

Christ asked Peter that question three times, because three times on the night he was crucified Peter had denied knowing Christ. Three times now Peter was forgiven for that hour of his human weakness, and three times Christ gave Peter a single directive for Peter's life. Then, Christ said to his disciples, "Follow me! For henceforth, all of you shall become fishers for the souls of people. All authority in heaven and on earth has been given to me. Therefore, go in my name and make disciples of all nations, baptizing them in the name of the Father and of the Son and of the Holy Spirit. And surely I will be with you always, to the very end of the age."

Christ then instructed his disciples to return to Jerusalem and wait for him there. After they had returned to Jerusalem, Christ appeared several times during the forty days following his resurrection. The people saw him, they touched him, they heard him speak, and they broke bread with him. In not one person was there any doubt that Christ was alive. After forty days had passed, Christ led those who were present out of Jerusalem to the Mount of Olives, where he prepared to depart from their midst. On this occasion Jesus instructed them all to return to Jerusalem and to wait there until the Holy Spirit descended on them.

They asked Christ, "Lord, are you at this time going to restore the kingdom to Israel?" Christ's reply to their question was, "It is not for you to know the time or dates the Father has set by his own authority. But you will receive power when the Holy Spirit comes on you, and you will be my witnesses in Jerusalem, and in all Judea, and Samaria, and to the ends of the earth." After he had said this, Christ was taken up before their eyes, until the clouds hid him from their sight.

Joseph of Arimathea was among those standing on the Mount of Olives when Christ departed from their midst. Afterwards, they returned to Jerusalem, many to their homes, some were guests of those who lived in that city, and others to their places of other lodging. The core group, however, which included "The Twelve," James and Joses, the brothers of Jesus, Mary their mother, and the other women, along with Joseph of Arimathea, went again to The Upper Room in obedience to Christ's command to wait until the promised Holy Spirit descended on them.

Each day thereafter they waited in hope for the Holy Spirit of which Christ spoke. They spend their day watching, waiting, praying, and encouraging each other to be patient. Each evening they retired wondering when the promised Holy Spirit would come. Then, on the tenth day following the ascension of Christ, on the very day when Pentecost had come, as they met again and prayed, suddenly and without warning a sound like the blowing of a violent wind came from heaven and filled the whole house where they were sitting. They saw what seemed to be a tongue of fire coming down and separating and coming to rest on each person there.

Suddenly, every person was caught in a euphoric experience whereby they began speaking in a language unknown to them. Many of them raced downstairs and into the street in that condition, where the passerby's thought they must be drunk. Peter explained that those on whom the Holy Spirit had descended were not drunk, but had been filled with the Glory of God from heaven. As Peter spoke, tongues of fire began touching those in the street, until the whole of all people in Jerusalem who would believe in Christ were touched by those tongues of heavenly power. Over three-thousand were added to their company of believers that day, and each day thereafter many others joined their fellowship.

Joseph of Arimathea was so much filled with joy that he did not think about it at the time, but later he said, "Let Caiaphas deal with this!" Nicodemus, who had been present and was also filled with the Holy Spirit, heard Joseph utter that statement.

Nicodemus discussed with Joseph of Arimathea how the earthly Jesus had once said to him, "Unless a man is born again, he cannot see the kingdom of God." Nicodemus said, "At the time, I asked Jesus if a man could enter again into his mother's womb to be born, and Jesus told me, 'Flesh gives birth to flesh, but the Spirit gives birth to spirit, so do not be surprised at my saying, you must be born again.' Now I understand what Jesus meant," said Nicodemus. "Truly, I have been born again; born this time of the Spirit who has given me a new birth of the spirit."

Then Nicodemus said, "When I was of the flesh, I hated Caiaphas, and everything he stood for. Now, having been born of the Spirit, I do not hate Caiaphas. I accept him, notwithstanding his arrogant attitude and his many faults. I accept him and I love him with this new love that has been given me. I still believe Caiaphas is wrong, and I have sensed for a long time that something was missing in the life of Caiaphas, as well as in my life. I could not pinpoint what was wrong, but in the new Spirit that has been given to me from heaven, I desire in love to persuade and win to Christ, not only Caiaphas, but all who follow him, that they may also be born from above. Love is the tool we have been given to win others into one great fellowship where the risen Christ is Lord."

Joseph and Nicodemus discussed this matter with the others, and from that time on they spoke a message of love, praying in love for their enemies; those who hated and despitefully used them. They believed all people were given a choice, and the choice they had made was the love with which Christ had, with his own life, surrendered, suffered, bled, and died, that by his example of love his followers would understand the proof of God's love for them. They decided that they could do no less, and love would be the message whereby they would call all people to repentance and the new birth.

In The Upper Room, they organized themselves in order to become more effective. Joseph of Arimathea and Nicodemus were both instrumental in helping them do this, calling upon their years of experience and explaining the values of organization. They drew lots to replace Judas Iscariot, the one who betrayed Jesus and who later hanged himself, and the lot fell upon Matthais. This brought their number again to twelve, and they busied themselves in serving the growing fellowship of believers.

Every day the Apostles would preach and exhort, comfort, feed, and heal. For relief in handling their many duties, they later chose seven others to assist them in the distribution of food. Each day they would pour into the Temple to worship and to bear witness to others who were gathered there. Daily they new converts were also united in their fellowship of believers.

It was then that Caiaphas and the chief priests began their tactics to divide and conquer. Economic sanctions were also brought to bear upon them. Many lost their jobs and livelihood because they belonged to the fellowship of believers. Others were required to leave their rented houses. The squeeze was on them to either relent or be ruined.

Peter and John were targeted for arrest and jailed, but they were delivered from their prison cell. The miraculous release of Peter and John from prison fueled the faith of the believers even more. Then Stephen, one of the seven, was arrested and stoned to death. Thereafter, members of the fellowship of believers realized their lives were in great jeopardy and many begin to flee Jerusalem for safer places. Their dispersion, however, unwittingly served to scatter beyond Jerusalem their message of Christ's resurrection and his redeeming love.

The message of Christ was not meant to be confined to Jerusalem; it was for all people throughout the whole wide world and, by the followers of Christ fleeing from Jerusalem, God was turning the tables on Caiaphas and the chief priests. By their actions, the seed of faith in Christ was being scattered abroad. This was only the beginning. The more tight Caiaphas and the Sanhedrin attempted to draw the noose around the ecstatic band of believers, the stronger and more faithful their fellowship grew.

That is when Joseph of Arimathea realized God's purpose for the great fortune with which he had been so wonderfully blessed. It was for such an hour and occasion as this. Joseph was already supplying some funds with which to purchase foodstuffs for the fellowship of believers in Jerusalem. Thus, he met with Peter and others to discuss the establishment of safe houses, not only at his home in Arimathea, but at Bethany, Jericho, Joppa and Sychar. It was indeed a blessing that Joseph possessed the financial means to assist in this decision.

Later, safe houses were also established in Caesarea, Tyre, Sidon, Damascus, Capernaum, Bethsaida, Seleucia, and Antioch. Several other places would later be established also, but Joseph never established a safe house in Nazareth. The House of David's royal family lived in Nazareth and Joseph hoped, in every possible way, to protect them. However, those same family members who lived in Nazareth were among the most ardent believers in the risen Christ, freely giving their support to the new Christian movement.

Joseph of Arimathea could not find a better way to use his wealth, and he was a blessing to the fellowship of believers. He explained all of this in a very long message to his son, Bran, who was in Seluria, England. He requested that Bran also share this information with his sister, Pernardim, with an emphasis that they should themselves believe in the risen Christ.

Joseph told his children that he would explain all this in greater detail when we returned to England, and that he would return there as quickly as possible, but for a time he believed it was imperative that he remain in Palestine to assist, in every possible way, the fledgling fellowship of believers in Christ. Joseph entrusted his message to Bran with his trusted servant, Elizar, sending him with detailed directions on his first voyage to England, where he was instructed to remain until Joseph arrived.

These early days of exciting, Spirit filled work and ministry quickly moved beyond Caiaphas and the chief priests of the Temple, establishing many house churches were the fellowships of believers met and broke bread together in worship and praise of Christ. The Twelve constantly traveled between house groups to minister, to preach, to exhort, to heal, and to baptize new believers.

Caiaphas and the chief priests continued to harass and punish those believers whom they caught, and believers had to remain constantly alert to avoid being captured. Later, word came that a man named Saul had been converted by the appearance of the risen Christ while he was traveling with an armed group and a warrant to arrest those believers who had fled Jerusalem to Damascus. Saul had been the chief official at the stoning to death of Stephen, but he was "converted" through the appearance of Christ, and a new word entered the language of the fellowship of believers.

Heretofore, the fellowship of believers had been identified as "Followers of The Way," but at Antioch they were called "Christians," and another new word was born and used by those who followed Christ. It made sense that they were "Christians," and that word became universally accepted as the one with which they would, henceforth, proudly identify themselves.

During the next 14 years Joseph of Arimathea made three voyages to England to visit his family. During his last five years in Palestine, he cared for Mary, the mother of Jesus, at his home in Arimathea. He was at her side when Mary died and, afterwards, Joseph carefully buried her body near his manor house. Upwards of six thousand people came to see her blessed body laid to rest.

Robert Cruikshank

In the same year that Jesus was crucified, his brother James was chosen by the Apostles to be bishop of the Church in Jerusalem. He remained in that position for twenty-nine years, until he was murdered in 62 A.D. Then Simeon, another brother of Jesus, took his place and, like James, rendered superb leadership to the Church in Jerusalem.

Chapter 18 – The Broader Vision

During those fourteen years after the crucifixion of Jesus, Joseph of Arimathea spent a sizeable portion of his fortune in support of the Christian movement. He thought it was money wisely invested. However, it was only a fraction of his usefulness in serving the new Church. In addition to establishing and funding the ongoing ministry where safe houses had been established and the people fed, his expertise was invaluable in every step of the Church's evolving organization and ministry. Joseph also played a large role in helping establish the early doctrines set forth by the Apostles, which they set forth in writing. They carefully made copies, providing them to every congregation.

Joseph supported Peter in opening the Church to receive Gentile converts into its fellowship. He continued to be an advocate for not requiring Gentiles first be circumcised before being admitted into Christian fellowship. His argument was that circumcision was a requirement of the old covenant which Christianity now superseded. Baptism was now the sign and ritual of the new covenant and the means of acceptance into full fellowship with other Christians.

Joseph's grandnephew, James, the brother of Jesus, who was now the bishop of Jerusalem, differed with Joseph on this matter. James was still holding on to the Temple, which he loved very dearly. James was also holding onto the old laws which he tenaciously observed. The Apostles, however, agreed with Peter and Joseph of Arimathea.

Gentile converts would be received into the Christian fellowship, and without first being circumcised. James eventually came to also fully accept this very important point.

The Church was enjoying great success outside Jerusalem in those days. Peter and the other Apostles were constantly going on a preaching mission to other areas to establish new churches and give guidance to their understanding of the new Church's doctrines, and to the practice of ministry with which to glorify Christ. The Jew formally named Saul, to whom Christ had appeared and converted on the Damascus road, changed his name to Paul of Tarsus and his missionary work was only beginning. Paul's fervor for Christ would soon greatly extend the scope of Christianity into Asia and the eastern part of Gaul.

Joseph of Arimathea was now ready to become Christianity's first missionary to England. With Mary the mother of Jesus having died, and with the work of the Church established throughout Palestine and the neighboring areas, there was no longer anything to keep him from fulfilling his long cherished desire of taking the message of Christ to England. He informed the Apostles of his heart's desire.

Peter and the other Apostles who were in Jerusalem at that time agreed they should send Joseph on a mission to England. They profusely thanked Joseph for the invaluable ministry and guidance he had rendered during these fourteen years. Then, they laid holy hands upon Joseph and blessed him for the mission to which they were sending him in England. They prayed that Almighty God in Christ, by the power of the Holy Spirit, would grant a bountiful harvest of new souls in that area which lay in the most extreme reaches of the Roman Empire.

At that time, Peter and the others also agreed to sent Philip on the first mission to Gaul (France). The day for their departure was set, and they were soon on their way to Joppa to arrange passage on a ship which could accommodate their number. As an Apostle, Philip headed the mission which included Joseph of Arimathea, along with twenty-two other brethren, of whom eleven were to remain with Philip for the work in Gaul, and eleven were to accompany Joseph into England. Lazarus, whom Jesus had raised from the dead, was one of those who would remain with Philip in Gaul

There were also several women among them, mostly wives of some of the men, in addition to those listed, which included Mary Magdalene, the most prominent personality among the women because she was with Jesus in the beginning and had remained his faithful servant all these years. She had helped Joseph care for Mary the mother of Jesus. So Mary Magdalene and Martha, the sister of Lazarus, having been blessed by Peter and the other Apostles, had been set apart as missionaries to Gaul. With Lazarus, these two planned to spend the remainder of their days as witnesses in service to the risen Christ among those Gentiles who resided in Gaul.

On this journey to England, Joseph of Arimathea took with him the exquisitely carved olive wood box containing the silver chalice with the blood of Jesus and the silver tray used by Jesus during the Last Supper.

Upon arriving in Gaul, landing at Marseilles, France, Lazarus was placed in charge of five other men, a group which included three of their wives, along with Mary Magdalene and Mary the sister of Lazarus. Philip and the others remained in Marseilles several days to see Lazarus and his group settled, then they sailed on to Burdigala (Bordeaux). There, Philip and the five men and four of their wives planned to establish there another mission for the cause of Christ.

After seven days Philip bade Joseph of Arimathea, and the eleven men who were to accompany him to England, to kneel and be blessed. On instructions from Peter and the other Apostles, Philip blessed them by the laying on of holy hands and also, at that time, anointed Joseph of Arimathea as the Apostle, sent to England by the grace of Almighty God to carry to the people who lived there the message of the resurrected Christ. It was a title Joseph had humbly refused in Jerusalem, feeling himself unworthy, but Peter and the others had directed Philip to bestow the title upon Joseph in token of their esteem for him, and in appreciation for his many years of faithful service to the cause of Christ. Joseph of Arimathea, now an Apostle, and as the newly appointed bishop of England, along with his twelve dedicated companions sailed for England on the evening tide.

With the establishment of these missions in Gaul and England, the Church at Jerusalem had truly become international, with a design to conquer the world through Christian love and service to others.

It was only natural that Joseph should be the one to head the first mission to Britain, and appropriate that he should come first to Glastonbury, that center for legendary activity in the West Country. Local legend has it that Joseph sailed around Land's End and headed for his old mining haunts. But his boat ran ashore in the Glastonbury Marshes and, together with his followers, he climbed a nearby hill to survey the surrounding area.

Cradled in one arm was the elegantly carved olive wood box which contained the silver chalice with the blood of Christ and the silver plate, both of which Jesus had used at the Last Supper in The Upper Room. In his other hand was a small staff fashioned from Christ's Holy Crown of Thorns. Being weary, Joseph and his eleven companions decided to sit and rest themselves for a time. Joseph thrust the staff from Christ's Holy Crown of Thorns into the ground and announced that he and his twelve companions were "Weary." The staff immediately took miraculous roots, grew, and the tree from which it grew can still be seen there on Weary Hill. Some soldiers chopped it down during Cromwell's Rebellion, but cuttings from the remaining roots continue to grow and blossom at Glastonbury to this day.

Joseph of Arimathea then met with King Arviragus, the local ruler, whom he had known for several years, and Joseph soon secured from Arvirgasus twelve hides of land at Ynys Vitrin (Glastonbury). On this piece of land they built a church of timber and wattles at the foot of the tor, naming it Saint Mary's Chapel, in honor of Mary the mother of Jesus, whom Joseph had so tenderly cared for at Arimathea during her declining years.

Joseph of Arimathea, the man who buried Jesus, was the first bishop and evangelist of the Christian gospel in England. He, who had been so instrumentally important during those early days of the Christian Church, served the gospel of Christ for another twenty years, dying at Glastonbury in A.D. 72, at the age of eighty-nine. He was buried in the church yard of St. Mary's Chapel. Buried with him, enfolded in his arms, was an exquisitely carved olive wood box. Inside the box was the silver chalice containing the blood of Christ, and the silver tray which Jesus had used on the night of his Last Supper.

The Holy Thorn, however, that tree which grew from a stick which Joseph of Arimathea had fashioned from the crown of thorns placed around the brow of Jesus, that thorny limb intended to make mockery of Jesus' kingship, still grows today at the site of where Saint Mary's Chapel once stood.

Every year, in late December, the Holy Thorn bursts forth with white, fragrant blossoms.

Chapter 19 – Followers of The Way

By the time of Joseph's death, most of the Apostles had been executed, along with hundreds of others who believed in the resurrected Christ. The cost of being a Christian was very high, and they were the martyrs of the faith. Still, the new birth in Christ having begun, burned brightly day and night.

They had no cloud of dust to lead them by day, and no pillar of fire to guide them by night as God had provided for his people on their journey from Egypt to the promised land. It was by faith that many thousands discovered a brighter, inner light, and a new, spiritual birth in Christ. Every day, throughout Palestine and the neighboring areas, many more continued to be added to their number.

One of them would express the common faith they shared, a belief they held that was more precious than mortal life itself: "That which was from the beginning, which we have heard, which we have seen with our eyes, which we have looked at and our hands have touched – this we proclaim concerning the Word of life. The life appeared; we have seen it and testify to it, and we proclaim to you the eternal life, which was with the Father and has appeared to us. We proclaim to you what we have seen and heard, so that you also may have fellowship with us. And our fellowship is with the Father and with his Son, Jesus Christ" (1 John 1:3).

Thus it was that, after Caiaphas and the Sanhedrin discovered they could neither subdue or destroy the Christians, those already hassled and harangued believers became easy prey and scapegoats for Rome's own degenerate failings. Beginning in the reign of the Emperor Nero and continuing for more than a hundred and fifty years Christian men and women were hauled into Roman arenas and used as sport for gladiators and food for the lions to pleasure a decadent and immoral generation.

Thousands would be condemned to die because of their faith, but those who opposed the Christ, like Caiaphas and other members of the Sanhedrin before them, were to learn that while they could kill Christians, they could neither destroy them nor subdue them, because those who lived and died in Christ already belonged to a kingdom far greater than this world could offer in exchange. Such was their faith in Christ, and love was the only witness they had with which to defend themselves.

The calling of Joseph of Arimathea as a missionary to England in A.D. 47, accompanied by his little band of eleven believers, was surely the foresight of God's wise mind in establishing Christianity as his new plan to bring his people of earth together into one wonderful, happy family. As God had previously raised up our fathers' Abraham, Isaac, Jacob, and David to lead his people in their assigned mission to the rest of his people, and with that mission having failed through disobedience and arrogance on the part of the Hebrew people, and even when God sent many prophets to warn the people they were treading on dangerous ground, they stoned and killed those sent to them.

When God sent his Son to renew and restore them into his grace, many of their leaders turned their backs on Christ, refused to receive him or believe him, then cruelly crucified him upon a cross at Calvary. The response of the Father of Christ was to raise his Son from the dead and to raise a new covenant people for his work on earth; those who believe in and follow God's Christ in faith and love. Those, and their descendants, who rejected Christ can at any time freely come to Christ and be freely forgiven and restored into the bosom of the Father.

The old covenant which generation after generation continuously presumed upon has been superseded by God's new covenant. A new covenant and a new people was set forth between his Christ and those who believe in, accept, and follow by faith the holy task of being his witnesses to all the world's people around the common table of God's uncommon love and grace.

God did not outright reject the old covenant with the Jewish people because the choice of free will and acceptance of the old covenant has always been ours to make. When under the old covenant we failed to fulfill our vows and duties, instead of outright cancellation of the old covenant, God made a new covenant which he invites us to accept. In effect, the old contract was made obsolete and a new one was offered to all who would repent of sin and receive into their hearts the love of God now shown in his begotten Son, Jesus the Christ. Every person is invited and this new covenant is between God and all his children of every nation. While there are many ways, this became, and remains The Way, and God's Way!

Neither did a holy God initiate a new covenant to see it smashed and destroyed during its early pains of birth. Every time the enemies of God attempted to destroy God's new covenant in one place, it would pop up in another place stronger then before. Nor did a righteous God revoke the free will of those who chose to oppose his new people and his new covenant, who chose instead to commit evil acts against his new people of his new covenant, but a persistent God ensured both their earthly and their heavenly survival.

With Joseph of Arimathea, God's plan was fully at work and at just the right time it would be revealed for all to see the genus of a just and holy God at work.

Among the converts to Christianity whom Joseph of Arimathea and his eleven brethren enrolled in their ledger was no other than King Arviragus and his wife Genvissa, the daughter of the Roman Emperor Claudius. Genvissa had married Arviragus at the time of Claudius' visit to England, as a means of assuring Arviragus' homage to Rome. During the twenty years that Joseph of Arimathea was bishop of England, many of the English people had embraced the

Christian faith, while many of those living in South Wales also became believers in Christ.

One way, among many, the providential arm of God ensured the survival of Christianity lay within the descendants of the family of Joseph of Arimathea. A crucial moment in the history of the Christian Church came when Constantine the Great, Emperor of Rome, a descendant of Anna and Joseph, gave Christianity a reception and standing throughout the Roman Empire.

Two hundred years and ten generations separated these two great followers of Christ, but they both served Christ with a faith passed down from parent to child with each generation embracing a new birth of love and service to Christ and their neighbor.

Joseph saw the risen Christ; Constantine saw a cross in the sky. Some scholars repeat what other scholars have said, telling us the cross in the sky was Constantine's moment of conversion. However, while the cross Constantine saw in the sky was for him a powerful and encouraging sign, as a child of his Christian mother, Helena, Constantine had been taught the history and prayers of his people along with the songs of their faith. She had taught Constantine, much like Moses had been taught by his mother, Jochebed, during the three or four years she had nursed him. When the time came for Moses to decide, his choice came easy because of his mother's teachings.

Likewise, Constantine was no stranger to Christ because his mother, too, had instilled in him the articles of faith whereby he easily recognized the sign of the cross in the sky and its meaning. He, too, had long before been prepared by a wise and loving mother, and by Almighty God, for that particular moment. Behind Constantine the Great stood ten generations of preparation for the task which almighty God was placing in his hand.

Those ten generations of Christian descent to Constantine the Great began with Anna and Joseph of Arimathea, who were the first generation.

In the second generation, Penardim of Siluria, daughter of Anna and Joseph of Arimathea and a first cousin of Mary and Joseph, was born in Palestine about B.C. 3. As a small child she was taken by her parents to England, probably around A.D. 2, where she grew to adulthood. She married Llyr Lediaith (aka Lear), son of Berwyn ap Ceri. Llry Lediaith was educated in Rome by Augustus Caesar. Their son was Bran ap Llry (also known as "Bran the Blessed Sovereign").

In the third generation, Bran ap Llry,(aka "Bran the Blessed Sovereign"). His wife's name was Enygeus, a descendant of Aedd Mawr (aka King Edward the Great). In the year A.D. 36, Bran ap Llry was commander of the British Fleet. As King of Siluria, he became the first royal convert to Christianity. When the Apostle Paul was a prisoner in Rome, Bran traveled there to provide him with assistance from his grandfather. Already a dedicated Christian, he was re-baptized by Paul, as was his son Caradoc and his grandsons Cyllin and Cynon, sons of Caradoc, who had already been taken to Rome. Within a few years after returning to England, Bran would resign the crown to his son and spend his remaining years advancing Christianity through England and Wales.

In the fourth generation, Caradoc ap Bran,(aka Caractacus), King of Siluria, was born at Trevan Llanilid, Glamorganshire, Wales. His main residence was at Abergwaredigion, "the Meeting-Place of the Saved/Released Ones." He was a hero of 40 battles. Tacitus, describing the stand made by the Silurians under Caradoc ap Bran at Caer Caradoc, near Knighton, states: "The intrepid countenances of their whole army and the spirit which animated them, struck the Roman commander, Ostorius, with astonishment . . . The chieftains of the various tribes were seen busy in every direction. They raced along the ranks of their army. They exhorted their warriors, they roused the timid, they inured the valient, and by promises inflamed the ardour of all. Caractacus was seen alternately in every part of his army. He galloped along the lines, exclaiming aloud: 'This day, my comrades, this very day, decides the fate of all Britain!'" Caradoc was expecting Gwyn to arrive with reinforcements, but they missed each other and while General Gwyn was conquering Caerwent, Caradoc was betrayed and captured by Argwedd Voeddig, Queen

Cartismandua of the north of England—a.k.a Brynack of the Britons and Brigante, the wife of Gwyn. In chains, Caradoc was handed a captive to the Roman General Ostorius Scapula. Caradoc and his sons Cyllin (aka Linus), Cynon, and his daughter Eurgain (aka Claudia), were afterwards placed in Rome, as hostages, in the care of Pomponia Graecenia, wife of the Roman Regent, General Plautus who had been commander in the invasion of AD 43. Pomponia was later charged at Rome with having "embraced a foreign superstition," having surely been led to belief in Christ by Cyllin (aka Linus), Cynon, and Eurgain (aka Claudia).

A interesting side note is that the Emperor Claudius adopted Eurgain and changes her name to Glaudia. She then married Rufus Prudens, the son of Aquila Prudentius, a Roman Senator and the husband of Priscilla. They are the Aquila and Priscilla mentioned by the Apostle Paul in Romans 16:3. Their son, Rufus, is also mentioned by Paul in Romans 16:13, saying "..his mother, who has been a mother to me, too" identifies Priscilla as also being Paul's mother, by a different father. Priscilla, Aquila, Prudens, Linus, and Claudia are further mentioned by Paul in 2 Timothy 4:21.

In the fifth generation, Cyllin ap Caradoc, (aka "St. Cyllin," and "Linus"), was sainted by the early Church of Britain. Both Morgan (1911) and Wurts (1942) write: "Linus and his sister Eurgain (aka Claudia) visited the Apostle Paul while he was a prisoner in Rome (2 Timothy 4:21). For some years after the death of Peter in A.D. 66 and Paul in A.D. 68, both Cyllin ap Caradoc, and Clement led their respective schools of Christianity at Rome. Eventually Cyllin ap Caradoc departed Rome to rejoin his royal kindred in Glamorgan, Wales, where he assumed the throne on behalf of his father during the remaining term of his father's "house arrest."

In generation six was born Coel ap Cyllin, (aka "Colilus I"), the son of St. Cyllin.. He is regarded by Dr. James Anderson as "Old King Coel." Of him, Morgan and Wurts say the name "Coel" implies the same meaning as the English name "Faith" does now. Coel ap Cyllin was educated in Rome.

In generation seven came Llew ap Coel, (aka "Lleuver Mawr," and "Lucius the Great"). He succeeded to the throne of Britain in 170 A.D. Of him, we are told his names,"Lucius the Great, or Lleuver Mawr, means "Great Luminary," and "Llew-ap-Coel" means "Benefit Son of Belief." He was the son of Coel ap Cyllin, and was baptized at Winchester by his father's first cousin St. Timothy, who suffered martyrdom at age 90 on 22 August 139. Lleuver died in 181. He married Gladys,daughter of Eurgen who was the daughter of Meric who married a daughter of Queen Boudecia.. Lleuver ap Coel founded the first church at Llandaff, changing the established religion there from Druidism to Christianity. Archbishop Stillingfleet states that the existence of King Lucius is proved, apart from the records of Wales, by two coins bearing his effigy, a cross, and the letters L.V.C. It appears that the succession to the throne, from Lucius, son of King Coel, had ended, but had been resumed in another line, descending from Owen, another son of Cyllin ap Caradoc, Owen being the brother of Coel.

In the eighth generation was born Gladys "the Younger," daughter of Llew ap Coel and Gladys; married Cadvan of Cambria, Prince of Wales, whose father was Iago. They were the parents of a son Cadwallow, and two daughters, Helena and Strada the Fair.

In the ninth generation, Helena verch Cadvan, (aka "Helen of the Cross," "Britannica," and "Flavia Julia Helena") was born in 248 at Drepanum in Bithynia, she died in 328, and was buried in Rome in the mausoleum near the Ss. Marcellino e Pietro at the Via Labicana. The porphyry sarcophagus, which contained her remains, is now in the Vatican Museum. She married Flavius Valerius Julius Constantius (aka Constantius), who was born 31 March 242. According to DiMaio (2003), "His family was from Illyricum and he was the son of Flavius Valerius Constantius, born 242, and Claudia, daughter of Claudius II." Constantius died 25 Jul 306 at Eboracum (York), England. He was a Roman Commander in England who became King of England by right of his wife, and later became also Emperor of Rome. In 327-328, after Helena's son, Constantine, became Emperor of Rome, she embarked on a pilgrimage to Palestine. With her son's assistance, they are said to have erected the "Church of the Resurrection" at the tomb of the Savior, and other magnificent churches at Bethlehem and on the Mount of Olives. Helena died in the presence of her son, Constantine, shortly after her pilgrimage because, as DiMaio (2003) suggests, "The abrupt interruption in the issue of Helena Augusta-coins in the spring of suggests, she died either at the end of 328 or the beginning of 329. Helena was made a saint in the a saint in the Roman Catholic Church, with her feast day being August 18. She was also made a saint In the Eastern Orthodox Church, with her feast day as May 21.

The tenth generation descendant of Anna and Joseph of Arimathea, was Flavius Valerius Aurelius Constantinus, (aka Constantine the Great). He was born in 27 February 265 at Naissua in the province of Moesia Superior of modern day Nish in Serbia. Constantine died in 336. He became the Emperor of Rome and is remembered as the Christian Emperor and who ended the era of Christian persecutions. He died, at the age of sixty-four years, on 22 May 337, at the palace of Achrrion, in the suburbs of Nicomedia, and was buried at Constantinople in his Church of the Apostles.

This was the family tree of Anna and Joseph of Arimathea:

1st Generation	Anna–Joseph of Arimathea
2nd Generation	Pernardim + Llyr Lediaith, and her brother *Bran (Beli) + Gladdys (see appendix)
3rd Generation	Bran ap Llry Lediaith (the Blessed Sovereign)
4th Generation	Caradoc ap Bran (Caractacus)
5th Generation	Cyllin ap Caradoc (St. Cyllin)
6th Generation	Coel ap Cyllin (Colilus I)
7th Generation	Llew ap Coel (Lucius the Great) + Gladys
8th Generation	Gladys "the Younger" verch Llew + Cadvan of Cambria
9th Generation	Helena verch Cadvan + Constantius
10th Generation	Constantine the Great

Joseph of Arimathea could not have foreseen that ten generations later the vine of his faith would bear fruit in the person of Constantine the Great. Joseph and Anna were faithful within their own generation, and that was sufficient. However, God had a longer view. He still does. Had Joseph of Arimathea failed to be faithful to the Christ, or had he chosen a different and easier path, without that spiritual linkage stretching to Helena, it is unlikely that Constantine would have become the person he was. What Joseph of Arimathea did by his faith was to make a difference to the world, even as we know it today. We, too, can make a difference because who and what we are today bears a hope and a legacy all its own, far beyond our own lives.

With Constantine, the carnage long waged against Christians was ended. Their undaunted faith in the Son of God, the risen Christ, by such persons as Joseph of Arimathea, Peter, Matthew, James, John, Paul, and thousands of unnamed other believers during those two-hundred and fifty years was fully justified. There were those who would destroy them and destroy the new covenant which God had divinely wrought, but God had his own plan to preserve his holy, begotten Church; a plan which God enacted through his servants from Joseph to Constantine, just as God had previously enacted another plan through his servant Moses and others.

Justice for God's Church and for God's new covenant people had finally arrived, yet their work was only beginning. During the ensuing years and centuries to come, there would be those who would from time to time misuse God's holy Church for personal gain and selfish ambition. As traitors to the cause of Christ, some would sell out their brothers and sisters. But the living body of Christ, not the institution itself, but those who repented of sin, believed in, loved, and lived in accord with those principles of acceptance and service to others in the name of Christ, would continue to bring glory, honor, and joy to the heart of Almighty God and to his Christ. And, in their sometimes sad and lonely hours, when Satan and the world seemed to gain the upper hand, the true believers knew, with their banners of faith flying, that God always has a better plan and he is working it out to perfection.

And the Holy Thorn at Glastonbury blooms every year, as an ever yielding testament to the faith of Joseph of Arimathea, and as a holy tribute to Christ, the Son of God, the Messiah who lives in the heart of every believer who chooses to live in love and service to others. It is the hope of Christ that all the people of earth will learn to fall in love again.

Chapter 20 – Epilogue

Much of the content of the foregoing chapters has been designed by the author to connect those dots of truth between known historical facts and ancient legends surrounding the life of Joseph of Arimathea. The facts themselves bear a resplendent testimony about his role and support in the formation of the Early Christian Church, and the advancement of the message of redemptive Christianity.

In the face of personal danger and against great odds, Joseph of Arimathea was, from the outset, a vital part in a community of believers whose faithfulness to the resurrected Son of God offered to all people a new life beyond the pale of mere mortal flesh and blood.

Theologians have long debated whether Joseph was a coward or a saint. There are some critics who have pointed out that, while Joseph was admittedly a disciple of Jesus, he was afraid to announce so publicly "because he feared the Jews" (John 19:38).

However, while Joseph of Arimathea may not have publicly revealed to Caiaphas and the Sanhedrin Council his own allegiance to Jesus during the earthly ministry of Jesus, there are two acts would seem to strongly place Joseph within that gallant category of "defender of the faith." One, Joseph of Arimathea was perhaps the sole member of the Sanhedrin who had opposed their decision and action regarding the arrest, trial, and crucifixion of Jesus (Luke

23:50-51). Two, following the crucifixion of Jesus, Joseph bravely went to Pilate, requesting the body of Jesus and, with Nicodemus, buried the body of Jesus according to Jewish burial customs (Luke 23:52-52). References to Joseph's actions may also be found in Matthew 27: 57-60, Mark 15:42-46, and John 19:38-42.

The facts are, according to scriptures, that in that darkness and gloom of those awful last hours of Jesus, his disciples having all forsaken him; Judas having sold him for thirty pieces of silver; the chief apostle Peter having denied him with a curse, swearing that he never knew Jesus; the chief priests having found Jesus guilty of blasphemy and the council having condemned Jesus to death; Joseph went against the powers that held the upper hand, and against the advice of his friends. Joseph begged Pilate for the body of Jesus and gave him a Jewish burial, laying the body of Jesus to rest in his own new tomb.

Other documents reveal how the Sanhedrin Council confronted Joseph of Arimathea that night for his actions of having buried Jesus according to Jewish custom. Joseph boldly accused the members of the Sanhedrin Council of killing the Messiah, and renounced them for their unrepentant action and behavior. The irate Council had Joseph arrested, placed him in a windowless cell, placed a seal upon the cell door, then placed two guards outside his sealed cell. When they returned, after the Sabbath was ended, Joseph of Arimathea was gone, but the seal mysteriously remained unbroken.

While serving Central Church in South Devon, at Torquay, England, as an exchange pastor, some of the church members took my wife and me by bus on a day trip to visit the cathedrals at Glastonbury and Wells. It was at Glastonbury that I encountered "The Holy Thorn" and the legend that Joseph of Arimathea had planted it there, then afterwards had constructed a church near that spot. I knew that my own genealogy was tied in there somewhere and the information from that unexpected encounter sparked in me an interest of research during the past twenty years.

Somewhere between the facts and legends lies my imagination of how things could have taken place and, while in this book I may have walked afield from the many events as they actually occurred, the conversations as they took place, the legends which are told, and even the facts which are accepted, I am confident in my heart that it issomething like that.

Anna knew beforehand that the Christ would soon reveal himself. She joined in faith with her niece and nephew, Mary and Joseph, in seeing from afar the coming of the Christ as the Son of God. Joseph of Arimathea, while also believing but still "not knowing," had an experience in which he saw the risen Christ who delivered him from his place of confinement where he had been placed by Caiaphas and other members of the Sanhedrin. Joseph of Arimathea , no doubt, also saw the risen Christ on other occasions, some of which are freely listed as some of Christ's appearances to Joseph and to others.

I, too, have seen the Christ. He appeared to me at seven minutes past midnight, the morning of 6 September 1952. I was visited by, and saw, the Lord in all his love and glory. For years I was fearful of telling anyone of my experience for fear they would think I was a prime case for the funny farm. When my experience was finally dragged out of me in an interview with a probing reporter, I found myself wonderfully relieved that my story was out. Now, like Joseph of Arimathea, I want to tell the whole wide world that Jesus lives!

Joseph of Arimathea, Nicodemus, Peter, and all those of the Early Church lived lives of faith and disciplined obedience to Christ. Because they believed, they were given an inner spiritual power with which to be reckoned. Yet, with all their faith and the power at their disposal, their desire was simple: it was to proclaim their oneness in Jesus Christ; it was to unite the world in love; it was to make this earth a place of peace and goodwill among all persons.

Their early desire and their ministry to others in the name of Christ, the Son of God, hve never gone out of style. It is the need today of all people of every nation:

–the need to be wanted.
–the need to be needed.
–the need to be accepted.
–the need to be secure.
–the need to be appreciated.
–the need to be rewarded.

Christians are people of faith. We believe and teach that the journey to oneness in the bonds of unity, love, peace and goodwill among all persons remains the one desire of almighty God; where Gentile and Jew, Christian and Muslim, Buddhist and Shinto, and all people of earth can gather at the common table of need, and find within our lives the blessed and the good we have inherited and can share together. These are one and the same hope for every person, and for all people.

We are also people of hope. Think about this: that there is the possibility there is now a small child in the city of Baghdad who is striving to survive the havoc presently being waged in that great city, who will in due time, emerge as a leader of that nation and lead the people there to new heights of reconciliation and wholeness, all of which is made possible by parents who believe this blessed hope, and will instill within their child the faith that clips the chain of sectarian division and makes hatred a thing of the past, embracing the unity essential for a life which bears the fruit of unity, peace, and goodwill under the umbrella of God's redeeming love.

We also have a choice. We are free to choose or to reject the great initiative of Almighty God in Jesus Christ to reclaim the many nations, cultures, and peoples of the world into one great fellowship of servant-believers. The many great belief systems of the world already share one thing in common, the love of Almighty God. Each of the world's religions does not have a different God. We acknowledge and share a belief in our God of redeeming love who is full of grace and mercy.

We acknowledge that God is our Creator, our Father, our Help, our Hope, our Glory, and our Eternal Home. It is incredulous then that, somehow, we should begin to think, in some quarters, that God is the Father of the Americans but not the Asians, or Africans. Or, that God is the Father of the Jews but not the Gentiles or the Arabs. Or, that God is Allah for the Islamic people but all other people, even deeply religious people, are infidels.

It is incredulous that any person of our heavenly Father should wish other persons of the heavenly Father be killed for being a so-called Infidel. instead of wishing them to be redeemed for the Glory of our heavenly Father. Many things just do not make sense; they just do not add up in any degree or the slightest trace of intelligence as conceived and applied to in our relationship with our heavenly Father and our fellow human beings.

God's Messiah, Jesus Christ, offers us a loving and intelligent way out of this practice of the world's religious madness, and we are all invited to choose this venue of divine love, forgiveness, and grace. God is already making the arrangements, a Father longing for every prodigal child, with the hope that we will come to our senses and find the way that leads us home.

If faith is the table at which we find acceptance, then love can be the pillow of our oneness in Almighty God.

Let us come and see!

Appendix

Some of the Descendants of Penardim, daughter of Anna and Joseph of Arimathea

1. JOSEPH of ARIMATHEA, married ANNA, daughter of Matthan and Hannah.
2. PENARDIM, the daughter of Joseph and Anna, married Llyr Lediath.
3. BRAN ap Llyr(aka "Bran the Blessed Sovereign"), King of Siluria, was the son of Penardim and Llye Lediath.
4. CARADOC ap BRAN (aka Caractacus).
5. CYLLIN ap CARADOC (aka St. Cyllin, and also called Linus), married Julia of the Iceni.
6. COEL ap CYLLIN (aka Colilus I), King of the Trinovantes.
7. LLEUVER ap COEL (aka Lleuver Mawr or Lucius the Great). His wife's name was Gladys the Elder.
8. GLADYS "THE YOUNGER," verch Lleuver and Gladys the Elder, married Cadvan of Cambria.
9. HELENA verch Cadvan (aka "Helen of the Cross," "Britannica" and "Flavia Julia Helena"), married Flavius Valerius Julius Constantius.
10. FLAVIUS VALERIUS AURELIUS CONSTANTINUS (aka Constantine the Great), Emperor of Rome, born 265, died 306. Of British birth and education, he is known as "The First" Christian Emperor. With a British army he set out to put down the persecution of Christians forever. The greatest of all the

Roman Emperors, he annexed Britain to the Roman Empire and founded Constantinople. In 325 he assembled the Council, which he attended in person, at Nicea in Bithynia, Asia Minor, which formulated the Nicene Creed. The following edict of Constantine clearly sets forth the standards of his life" "We call God to witness, the Savior of all men, that in assuming the government we are influenced solely by these two considerations, the uniting of the empire in one faith, and the restoration of peace to a world rent in pieces by the insanity of religious persecution". He had three sons, [1] Constantine II, [2] Constantious II and [3]Constans I. It is said that his eldest son, Constantine II, was the father of Uther Pendragon, who became King of Britain in 498. Uther Pendragon's son, King Arthur, succeeded his father in the year 516 at the age of 15, repulsed the invading Saxons and died 21 May 542. Arthur is most best known in connection with his Knights of the Round Table. His body rests beside his wife, Guinevere, in a tomb at Glastonbury.

11. FLAVIUS IAVIUS JULIUS CONSTANS,(aka CONSTANS I), reigned over two-thirds of his father's empire. He was slain in A.D. 350. Then follows those descendants, each numbered in turn . . . :

12. PIRCAMESSER
13. SLATER
14. ELIUS
15. ELOUID
16. YTECTOR
17. YTEC
18. MAXIM GUELETIC
19. DIMET
20. NIMET
221. GLOTGUIN

22. CLOTRI
23. TRIFUN
24. AIRCOL
25. GUERTENIR
26. CINCAR
27. PETR
28. ARTHUR
29. MOUGOY
30. CLOTEN
31. CATGOCAUM

32. REGIM
33. TEUDOS
34. MARGETUIT
35. OVEL
36. TANCOYST
37. HYMEYT
38. LLYWARCH, Prince of Wales
39. ELENA, married Dha (Hywel the Good ap Cadwell) grandson of Rhodri Mawr.

40. OWEN, Prince of South Wales, married Ankaret Queen of Powys (his 2nd Cousin).
41. MAREDYDD, Prince of Powys, died 999, married Asritha, They were the parents of a daughter, Angharad.

42. ANGHARAD verch Maredydd, Queen of Powys; married Llwellyn ap Seisyll, Prince of North Wales.

43. GRYFFYDD ap LLWELLYN, (aka Griffet), died 5 Aug 1063, married Eldgyth (Edith) "Swan Neck" verch Gruffydd Malet.

44. NESTA verch GRYFFYDD, married Osbern Fitz-Richard of Scrob.

45. AGNES verch OSBERN FITZ-RICHARD, married Bernard de Newmarch, Lord Brecon.

46. SYBIL de NEWMARCH, married in 1121 to Miles Fitz-Walter de Petris, Earl of Gloucester and Earl of Hereford.

47. BERTHA of GLOUCESTER, married William de Braose, Baron of Gwent, son of Philip de Braose and Aenor de Totnais.

48. WILLLIAM de BRAOSE, married Maud de St. Valery, Lady of Haye. She and a son William were starved to death at Windsor Castle in 1210. Another son was:

49. REGINALD de BRAOSE, died in 1210, married Graecia (or Grisold) de Briwere, daughter and co-heir of William de Briwere.

50. WILLIAM de BRAOSE, of Brecknock, Lord of Abergavenny, married Eva Marshall, daughter of William Marshall, Earl of Pembroke, and his wife Isabel de Clare.

51. ELEANOR de BRAOSE, married Humphrey de Bohun VI, son of Humphrey de Bohun V and his wife Maud d'Eu Lusignan

52. HUMPHREY de BOHUN VII, Earl of Herefore and 2nd Earl of Essex, married Maud d'Fienes, daughter of William d'Fienes Enguerrand and his wife Maud Hampden.

53. HUMPHREY de BOHUN VIII, 4th Earl of Hereford and 3rd Earl of Essex, Lord of Brecknock, Lord High Constable of England, born 1276, killed at Buroughbridge and buried in Friars Preachers Church, York; married 14 Nov 1302 Elizabeth Plantagenet, Princess of England, born 5 Aug 1282 at Rhuddlan Castle, Co. Flint—died 5 May 1316, buried at Walden Priory, 9th daughter of King Edward 1st and Eleanor of Castile, and widow of John 1st, Count of Holland and Zealand. The effigy and tomb of Humphrey de Bohum VIII and Elizabeth Plantagenet now lie in the south aisle, next to the choir, at Exeter Cathedral, Exeter, Devon, England. Two of their children included: i. William de Bohun, K.G., 1311-1360. ii. Margaret de Bohun, born 3 Apr

1311, died 16 Dec 1391 (listed below), married Sir Hugh de Courtenay.

54. WILLIAM de BOHUN, K.G., 1311–1360, 1st Earl of Northampton,; married Elizabeth de Badlesmere, 1313–1355; widow of Edmund Mortimer and daughter co-heiress of Bartholomew de Badlesmere, Lord Badlesmere of Leeds Castle, and his wife Margaret de Clare, daughter of Thomas de Clare and Julian Fitz-Maurice (who was the daughter of Maurice Fitz-Maurice, Lord Justice of Ireland).

55. ELIZABETH de BOHUN, born/abt. 1350 Derbyshire, England, died 3 Apr 1385 Arundel Castle, Sussex, England, married Richard FitzAlan, K.G., born 1346 Arundel Castle, Sussex, England, executed 21 Sep 1397, 10th Earl of Arundel, Earl of Surrey, and Admiral of the Fleet. Failing in his opposition to the Duke of Lancaster and Richard II, he was beheaded in 1397, at Cheapside, London, England. He was the son of Sir Richard Fitz Alan and Eleanor Plantagenet.

56. JOAN FITZ ALAN, born/abt. 1365 Arundel Castle, Sussex, England, died 14 Nov 1435, England, married/ab1380 to William de Beauchamp, K.G., Justiciar of South Wales and Governor of Pembroke, born 1358 Warwick Castle, Warwickshire, England, died 8 May 1411, England.

57. RICHARD de BEAUCHAMP, K.G., died 1422, Lord Abergavenny, Earl of Worcester, married Isabel le Despenser, daughter of Thomas le Despenser and Constance Plantagenet. Isabel le Despenser married 2nd a first cousin of her 1st husband, also named Richard de Beauchamp (aka "Kingmaker"), son of Thomas de Beauchamp.

58. ELIZABETH de BEAUCHAMP, born 16 Sep 1415–died 18 Jun 1488, Baroness Abergavenny, only daughter and heiress of Richard de Beauchamp, K.G.; married Edward de Neville, K.G., Lord Abergavenny, son of Ralph de Neville, 1st Earl of Westmoreland by his 2nd wife Joan de Beaufort, Dowager Lady Ferrers de Wemme, the legitimated daughter of John of Gaunt, Duke of Lancaster (son of King Edward III), and Gaunt's 3rd wife, Katherine Swynford.

59. GEORGE de NEVILLE, Knt., born circa 1440 at Raby Castle–died 20 September 1492, Lord Burgevenny, M.P. 1482-1492, son of Edward de Neville and Elizabeth de Beauchamp; married 1st Margaret Fenne, died 28 Sep tember 1485, daughter and heiress of Sir Hugh Fenne, of Sculton Burdeleys and Norfolk, and Treasurer of the Household to King Henry IV.

60. GEORGE de NEVILLE, K.B., K.G., died 1535, Lord Burgavenny, Privy Councillor, son of George de Neville and Margaret Fenne; married 3rd Mary de Stafford, daughter of Edward de Stafford, K.G., 3rd Duke of Buckingham, and his wife Eleanor de Percy, daughter of Henry de Percy, 4th Earl of Northumberland, and Lady Maud Herbert.

61. URSULA de NEVILLE, Obit. 1575, buried in sepulcher at Ulcombe Church, in Kent, 5th daughter of George de Neville and Mary de Stafford, married Sir Warham St. Leger, of Ulcombe and Leeds Castle, Kent, 1559 Sheriff of Kent, 1565 Knighted, 1565 President of Munster in Ireland, Obit. 1597 in Cork, Ireland. His will is in the Heralds' College, London, England. It should be noted that many of the ancestral lines of Biblical and Ancient times culminate in Ursula St. Leger, with one line of her descendants catalogued through her son, Sir Anthony St. Leger, as follows:

62. ANTHONY ST. LEGER, Knt., of Ulcombe, Kent, born 1578-died 1603; married circa 1578 to Mary Scott, died 1636, daughter of Sir Thomas Scott. Sir Anthony St. Leger came to America in 1609, was a personal friend of Sir Walter Raleigh. Sir Anthony became a member of the Virginia House of Burgesses. He later returned to England and became the Lord Mayor of London.

63. WARHAM ST. LEGER, Knt., of Ulcombe, Kent, died 10 Nov 1631; married Mary Hayward, died 1662, daughter of Sir Rowland Hayward, Knt., Lord Mayor of London, and his wife Joan, daughter and heiress of William Tylifworth. Their daughter was:

64. MARY ST. LEGER, born at Ulcombe, Kent, England in1612; married in January 1633 license issued 27 November 1632) to Col. William Codd, Esq., of Pelicans in Wateringbury, Kent, England, where a brass in his honor exists in the Wateringbury

Church. His Will, dated 16 Dec 1652, proved 25 July 1653, is published in The Virginia Historical Magazine, Vol. 23, page 382-3, 1915, naming his wife Mary, eldest son Saint Leger Codd, sons Anthony and Rowland, and daughters Mary, Barbara, Deborah, Katherine, Elizabeth, and Anne.

65. COLONEL St. LEGER CODD, Emigrant to America from England, was born circa 1636 at Pelicans of Wateringbury, Kent, England. He married four times; 1st on 18 May 1667, in England, to Beatrice Pitt, daughter of Ann Pitt. They had no children; 2nd about 1668, in the year he came to Virginia, to Mrs. Anne Mottrom Wright Fox (widow of 1st Richard Wright and 2nd David Fox). She was the daughter of Col. James Mottron. To St. Leger Codd and Anne Mottrom Wright Fox were born two sons, James Codd and Berkeley Codd. His 3rd marriage, in 1671, was to Mrs. Anna Bennett Bland,. She was born in 1641 in Virginia, died November 1687 at Warton Creek Manor, Warton Creek, Maryland, and was the widow of Governor Theodoric Bland and the daughter of Governor Richard Bennett). To St. Leger Codd and Anna Bennett Bland Codd was born a son, Captain St. Leger Codd, and two daughters, Beatrix and Sara Codd. His 4th marriage was to a widow, Anna Hynson Randall Wickes. They had no children. Colonel St. Leger Codd arrived in Virginia circa 1668, settling at Wicomico, Northumberland County. He was one of the Commissioners appointed to superintend the building of a fort on the Potomac in 1671, was listed as Colonel of the Northumberland County Militia in 1676. He was named as a Justice in 1677, Presiding Justice in 1680, Member of the House of Burgesses 1680 and 1682. Soon thereafter he removed to Maryland, where he is listed in the Calendar of State Papers, Colonial Series, America and West Indies, 1689-1692, as among the list of names of substantial Protestants submitted by Lord Baltimore to the Council of Maryland. His name appears again in the State papers for 1696-1697 , as Justice of the Provencial Court. In 1701 he was listed as Member of the State Assembly from Cecil County. His will, dated 7 Nov 1706, was proved in Maryland on 9 Feb 1707/8 and also in Lancaster, Virginia, on 8 Apr 1708. He was buried

in St. Paul's church- yard, Kent County, Maryland (St. Paul's Register, page 252, at St. Mary's, Kent County, Maryland.

66. CAPT. ST. LEGER CODD, born 16 Dec 1680 in Northumberland County, Virginia, and died in 1732 in Cecil County, Maryland. He was a Captain in the Maryland militia and a member of the Maryland legislature from Cecil County from 1712-1716 and, again, from 1719-1720 (The Virginia Historical Magazine, Vol. 10, page 373-5, 1902). He married in 1709, in Maryland, to Mary Hanson, born 16 Dec 1680 in Kent Co., Maryland, died 1732 in Cecil Co., Maryland. She was the daughter of Hans Hanson and Martha Woodard. Captain St. Leger Codd and Mary Hanson were the parents of three daughters, viz., Ann, Mary Ann, and Beatrice.

67. MARY ANN CODD, born 1710 in Kent Co., Delaware, died 1755 in Hopewell, New Jersey; married on 21 February 1730 in St. Paul's Parish, Kent Co., Maryland, to James Stout, born 1701 in New Jersey, and died 1775 at Hopewell, New Jersey, son of Joseph Stout and Ruth Brinson.(See Chapter 45 for the Stout Family Threads). Their son was:

68. St. LEGER CODD STOUT, born 2 January 1731 at Amwell, New Jersey, died 10 February 1767 at Amwell, New Jersey; married in N.J. to Susannah Simpson. She was born 1735 in New Jersey, and died 8 February 1770 in New Jersey. Their children were:
i. Nancy Ann Stout, born 25 July 1756, died 25 February 1844.
ii. St. Leger Stout, Jr.

69. NANCY ANN STOUT, was born 25 July 1756 in New Jersey, died 25 February 1844 in Beverly, Randolph Co., West Virginia. She married in October 1777 in Hunterdon Co., New Jersey, to Edward Hart, born 20 December 1755 in Hopewell, New Jersey, died 5 October 1812 in Beverly, Randolph Co., Va.(now WV), son of John Hart and Deborah Scudder. Edward Hart was a soldier in the American Revolution in New Jersey's "Hunt's Militia," and his father, John Hart, was a delegate from New Jersey to the Continental Congress and a Signer of the Declaration of Independence. Edward and Nancy Stout Hart are buried in the Beverly Cemetery, Beverly, WV. They

were the parents of five daughters and four sons, including a daughter:

70. SUSANNAH HART, born 14 February1782 in Hopewell, New Jersey,, died 1 July 1843 in Logansport, Cass Co., Indiana. She married George Washington Stalnaker on 17 November 1796 in Beverly, Randolph Co.,Va. (now WV). He was born 27 February 1777 in Beverly, Randolph Co., Va. (now WV), and died 14 November 1857 in Logansport, Cass Co., Indiana, son of Valentine Stalnaker and Catherine Marteney. They are buried in Lot 238, 9th Street Cemetery, Logansport, Indiana. They were the parents of five daughters and four sons, one son being:

71. JOHN STALNAKER, born 6 November, 1804 at Beverly, Randolph Co., Va. (now West Virginia), died 30 March 1862 at Reedy, Roane Co., West Virginia. On 19 November 1830 at Beverly, Randolph Co.,Va. (Now WV), he married Susanne Chenoweth, born 29 April 1812 at Beverly, Randolph Co., Va. (now WV), died 20 April 1862 at Reedy, Roane Co., WV, daughter of Robert Chenoweth and Edith Skidmore. They were the parents of four daughters and two sons, including:

72. MARTHA ANN STALNAKER, born 1 Feb 1834, at Beverly, Randolph Co., Va. (now WV), died 15 Sep 1870 on Cox`s Fork, Harper Dist., Roane Co., West Virginia. She married on 19 June 1851 in Wirt Co., Va. (now WV) to Robert Hopkins, born 23 Dec 1822, Pendleton Co., Va (now WV), died 10 Feb 1894, at Round Knob, Roane Co., WV, son of Lawrence Braddock Hopkins and Mary "Polly" Jordan. They were the parents of 4 daughters and 4 sons, including:

73. ALBERT JENNINGS FLOYD HOPKINS, born 17 Jul 1862 on Flat Fork, Harper Dist., Roane Co., WV, died 03 Mar 1938 at Wanego, Geary Dist., Roane Co., WV. He married , 30 Dec 1885 at Wanego, Geary Dist., Roane Co., WV, to Martha Marcina Gandee, born 23 Nov 1866 at Gandeeville, Roane Co., WV, died 13 Nov 1946 at Wanego (now Newton), Roane Co., WV, daughter of Frederick Gandee and Caroline Canterbury. The only son of Floyd Hopkins and Martha Gandee was:

74. ROBERT FREDRICK HOPKINS, born 09 Sep 1890 in Wanego (Newton P.O.), Geary Dist., Roane Co., WV, died 29 May 1953 in Charleston, Kanawha Co., WV. He married 17 Jul 1911 at Bloomington, Roane Co., WV, to Nora Catherine Cook, born 28 Oct 1892 at Bloomington (Amma P.O.), Geary Dist., Roane Co., WV, died 05 Jan 1969 in Charleston, Kanawha Co., WV, daughter of Aaron Cook and Mary D. M. Drake. They were the parents of 3 daughters and 3 sons, including:

75. THELMA EVELYN HOPKINS, born 16 Aug 1912 in Bloomington (Amma P.O.), Geary Dist., Roane Co., WV, died 17 Oct 1979 in Orrville, Wayne Co., Ohio. She married on 20 Apr 1930 at Clendenin, Kanawha Co., WV, (license issued Roane Co.), to Gerald Leo Cruikshank, Sr., born 08 Mar 1908 in Middle Creek, Clay Co., WV, died 17 Aug 1971 in the VA Hospital, Huntington, Wayne Co., WV, son of Oscar Evert Cruikshank and Lois Elvina Morton.

More Descendants of Penardim, daughter of Anna and Joseph of Arimathea, continuing from Generation 53, above, as follows:

53. HUMPHREY de BOHUN VIII, 4th Earl of Hereford and 3rd Earl of Essex, Lord of Brecknock, Lord High Constable of England, born 1276, killed at Buroughbridge and buried in Friars Preachers Church, York; married 14 Nov 1302 to Elizabeth Plantagenet, Princess of England, born 5 Aug 1282 at Rhuddlan Castle, Co. Flint, died 5 May 1316, buried at Walden Priory, 9th daughter of King Edward 1st and Eleanor of Castile, and widow of John 1st, Count of Holland and Zealand. The effigy and tomb of Humphrey de Bohum VIII and Elizabeth Plantagenet now lie in the south aisle, next to the choir, at Exeter Cathedral, Exeter, Devon, England. Two of their children included: i. William de Bohun, K.G., 1311-1360 (listed previously, above). ii. Margaret de Bohun, born 3 Apr 1311, died 16 Dec 1391; married Sir Hugh de Courtenay (as shown next . . .)

54. MARGARET de BOHUN, born 3 Apr 1311 in Caldecote, Northamptonshire, England, died 16 Dec1391 in Exeter, Devonshire, England; married 11 Aug 1325 HUGH DE

COURTENAY. Their magnificent side-by-side tombs are located in Exeter Cathedral, Exeter, Devonshire, England.

55. PHILIP COURTENAY, born/abt. 1346 in Exeter, Devonshire, England, died 29 Jul 1406; married/abt. 1380 to Anne Wake, born/abt. 1360 in Northamptonshire, England, died 1390.

56. JOHN COURTENAY, born/abt. 1384, died/bef. 29 Jul 1406; married/abt. 1403 to JOAN CHAMPENON, born/abt. 1382, died 1419.

57. PHILIP COURTENAY, born/abt. 1404 in Powderham Castle, Devonshire, England, died 16 Dec 1463; married/abt. 1425 to ELIZABETH HUNGERFORD, born/abt. 1400, died 14 Dec 1476.

58. WILLIAM COURTENAY, born/abt. 1428 in Powderham Castle, Devonshire, England, died Sep 1485 in Powderham Castle, Devonshire, England; married/abt. 1450 to MARGARET BONVILLE, born/abt. 1432, died/bef. July 1487 at Powderham Castle, Devonshire, England.

59. EDWARD COURTENAY, born/abt. 1453, died 1 Mar 1506 in Landrake, Cornwall, England; married/abt. 1483 to ALICE WOTTON, born/abt. 1473, died 29 Sep 1533.

60. EDWARD COURTENAY, born 1495; married MARGARET (JANE) THETFORD, born 1505, died 18 Jun 1576.

61. PETER COURTENAY, born 1536, died 28 May 1606, married KATHERINE RESKYMER, born 1546, daughter of William Reskymer and Alice Densell.

62. ANN COURTENAY, born Vrottonin, Cornwall, England; married GILBERT HOLCOMBE, born 1565 at Hole, Devonshire, England, died/bet. 1633-1634 in Pembroke, Pembrokeshire, Wales, son of Thomas Holcombe and Margaret Trethford.

63. THOMAS HOLCOMBE, born 1595 in Hole, Devonshire, England, immigrated to America and died 1657 at Windsor, Connecticut; married/abt. 1632 at Dorchester, Massachussets, to ELIZABETH FERGUSON, born in Wales, died 7 Oct 1679 at Simsbury, Connecticut.

64. JOSHUA HOLCOMB, born 7 Apr 1640 at Windsor, Connecticut, died 1 Dec 1690 at Simsbury, Connecticut, married 4 Jun 1663 at Windsor. Connecticut, to RUTH SHERWOOD, born in

Massachusetts and died 10 Sep 1699at Simsbury, Connecticut, daughter of Thomas and Mary Sherwood.

65. JOSHUA HOLCOMB II, born 18 Sep 1672 at Simsbury, Connecticut, died 10 Feb 1725 at Simsbury, Connecticut, married (1st) in 1694 at Simsbury, Connecticut, to HANNAH CARRINGTON, born 1675, died 13 May 1708 at Simsbury, Connecticut; married (2nd) abt. 1709 to Mary Hoskins.

66. JOSHUA HOLCOMB III, born 18 Sep 1697 in Fairfield County, Connecticut, died Nov 1772; married/abt. 1720 at Simsbury, Connecticut, to MARY GRIFFIN, born 16 Sep 1699, daughter of Thomas Griffin and Elizabeth Welton.

66. HEZEKIAH HOLCOMB, born 3 Jan 1725 at Simsbury, Connecticut, died/unk. at Bloomfield, Connecticut; married on 29 Sep 1748 at Simsbury, Connecticut, to SUSANNAH ALDERMAN, born 5 Sep 1728, died 1814 at Bloomfield, Connecticut, daughter of Josiah Alderman and Mindwell Case. Hezekiah Holcomb was a soldier in the American Revoluttionary War, serving as Captain, 18th Conn. Regt. & 11th Conn. Regt.

67. TIMOTHY HOLCOMB, born 25 Feb 1756 in Connecticut, died/ aft. 1844 in Highland County, Virginia, (now Pocahontas County, West Virginia; married ELIZABETH GRIFFIN, born 26 May 1755 in Connecticut, died/aft. 12 Apr 1808 in Pocahontas County, Virginia (now WV). Timothy Holcomb served during the Revolutionary War as a Lieutenant in Colonel Hizman's 4th Conn. Regt.

68. ETHAN ALLAN HOLCOMB, born 1789 in Connecticut, died/ unk., married SUSAN HUGHES, born 1794 in Virginia. They were living in Clay County at the time of the 1860 Federal Census, Ethan age 72, Susanage age 67.

69. EZEKIEL HOLCOMB, born 1812 in Virginia (now West Virginia), died/abt 1865 in Belle Isle or Libby Prison, a Civil War POW. He married/abt. 1834 in Nicholas Co., Virginia (now West Virginia) to RACHAEL NEAL, born 1810 in Nicholas County, Virginia (now West Virginia), died/unk. Clay County, West Virginia, daughter of John Neal and Ann O'Dell.

70. ETHAN ALLAN HOLCOMB II, born Aug 1834 in Nicholas County, Virginia (now WV), died 21 Jan 1858 in Clay County, West

Virginia; married 21 Jan 1858 in Clay County to ANNA LOUISE RAMSEY, born Dec 1838 at Ramsey, Fayette County, Virginia (now WV), died 20 Dec 1919 in Clay County, West Virginia, daughter of Abner Ramsey and Martha Hawkins. Ethan Allan Holcomb II was a Union Soldier during the Civil War and was returning home on furlough, along with his father and two other Union soldiers, when they were ambushed by Confederates. He was wounded and left for dead and his father was taken prisoner. He recovered from his wounds but his father died in a Confederate prison camp.

71. JULIA ANN HOLCOMB, born 21 Nov 1858 at Fola, Clay County, West Virginia, died 17 March 1947 at Lizemores, Clay County, West Virginia; married 23 Apr 1885 at the home of her parents in Clay County, West Virginia, to Rev. John T. Morton (she was his 4th wife), He was born 20 Jul 1823 in Nicholas County, West Virginia, died 1913 in Clay County, West Virginia, son of Thomas T. Morton (Throckmorton) and Amelia Young. John T. Morton was a Union soldier during the Civil War. He was a Justice in Nicholas County, then in Clay County when that county was formed. He also served on the Clay County School Board. He built his own grist mill, and was also an expert carpenter and blacksmith. On 2 Sep 1865 he received a Exhorter's License in the Methodist Episcopal Church, and a Local Preacher's License on 1 Sep 1866 at the Quarterly Conference of the Charleston District, West Virginia Conference Methodist Episcopal Church.

71. LOIS ELVINA MORTON, born 6 January 1893 at Lizemores, Clay County, West Virginia, died there 27 November 1948; married 1 Nov 1905 at Charleston, Kanawha County, West Virginia, to OSCAR EVERT CRUIKSHANK, born 10 Jan 1883 at Zela, Nicholas County, West Virginia, died 18 Jun 1955 at Charleston, Kanawha County, West Virginia, son of William Madison Crookshanks and Nancy Eveline Fitzwater. He was a descendant of John Crookshanks of Augusta Co., Va., who was a soldier of the American Revolutionary War, serving in the 10th and 6th Virginia Regiments, and was with Washington at Valley Forge and in the Battles of Brandywine, Georgetown,

and Germantown, before being wounded in the knee during the Battle of Guilford Courthouse (now Greensboro), North Carolina.

72.   GERALD LEO CRUIKSHANK, Sr., born 8 Mar 1908 in Clay County, West Virginia, died 17 Aug 1971 at Huntington, Wayne County, West Virginia; married 20 Apr 1930 at Clendenin, Kanawha County, West Virginia, to Thelma Evelyn Hopkins, born 16 Aug 1912 in Roane County, West Virginia, died 17 Oct 1979 at Orrville, Wayne County, Ohio.

Note: The above persons at Generation #72, are the same as those persons listed as Generation #75 in the shown line of descendants from Penardim, daughter of Anna and Joseph of Arimathea.

SOME OF THE DESCENDANTS OF BRAN (aka BELI),
SON OF ANNA AND JOSEPH OF ARIMATHEA

1.   JOSEPH of ARIMATHEA, married ANNA. Their son was was Bran (aka Beli).
2.   BRAN (aka Beli)
3.   AMALECH ap BELI.
4.   ABALLAC ap AMALECH.
5.   EUGENE ap ABALLAC.
6.   BRITHGUEIN ap EUGENE.
7.   DUBUN ap BRITHGUEIN.
8.   OUMAN ap DUBUN.
9.   ANGUERIT ap OUMAN.
10.   AMGUOLOYT ap ANGUERIT.
11.   GURDUMN ap AMGUOLOTY.
12.   DUMN ap GURDUMN.
13.   GUORDOLI ap DUMN.
14.   DOLI ap GUORDOLI.
15.   GUROCEIN ap DOLI.
16.   CEIN ap GUROCEIN.
17.   TEGIDP ap CEIN, b/abt. 314 in Wales.
18.   PADARN ap TEGIDP, b/abt. 339 in Wales.

19. EDERN ap PADARN, b/abt. 364 in Wales.

20. CUNEDDA "WEIDIG" ap EDERN, King of Wales, born/aft. A.D. 386 in Cardigen, Wales,died/abt. A.D. 440; Gwawl verch Coel, b/abt. 388 in Wales.

21. EINION "YRTH' ap CUNEDDA, King of Gwynedd, b. 417 in North Wales; married Prawst verch Tidlet, b/abt. 422 in Powys, Wales.

22. CADWALLON "LAWHIR" ap EINION, Prince of North Wales, b/abt. 442 in Wales; married Meddyl verch Maeldaf, b/abt. 446 in Nanconwy, Arlfechwedd, Carneavon- shire, Wales.

23. MAELGWYN "GWYNEDD" (aka Melgo) ap CADWALLON, King of Gwynedd, b/abt. 470 in North Wales, died abt. 550; married Gwellwen verch Afallach, b/abt. 471.

24. RHUN "HIP" ap MAELGWYN, King of Gwynedd, b/abt. 490 in North Wales, died 584; married Perwry verch Rhun, b/abt. 496.

25. BELI ap RHUN, King of Gwynedd & Prince of North Wales, b/abt. 517, died 598.

26. IAGO ap BELI, King of Gwynedd, b/abt. 540, died 616. Geoffrey of Monmouth says that Iago inherited the kingship of Gwynedd but abdicated in favor of his son, Cadvan, and became a monk.

27. CADVAN ap IAGO, King of Gwynedd & Prince of Wales, b/abt. 569, died 630. He married Tamdred "Ddu" verch Cynon, b/abt. 569 in Powys, Wales.

28. CADWALLON ap CADVAN, King of Gwynedd & Prince of Wales, b/abt. 591, died 635 (killed in battle); married the daughter of Pybba, b/abt 594 in Mercia, England.

29. CADWALLADER "FENDIGAID" ap CADWALLON, the 3rd Blessed Sovereign, King of Gwynedd & Prince of Wales, b/abt. 615 in Wales, died of the plague in 664. was the last king of the ancient Britons.

30. IDWAL "YWRCH" ap CADWALLADER 'FENDIGAID," Prince of North Wales, ruled over Anglesey, b/abt. 664, died 712. He married Agatha, Countess of Brittany, daughter of Alan, Count of Brittany.

31. RHODRI "MOLWYNOG" ap IDWAL, Prince of North Wales, b/abt. 664, died 754, ruled over Anglesey 720-754, married Margaret, daughter of Duptory, King of Ireland.

32. CYNAN "DINDAETHWY" ap RHODRI, became the King of Wales, b/abt. 754, died 817, was the Ruler of Triudaethwy 755-817. He married Matilda, Countess of Flint, whosd father was the Earl of Flint.

33. ESSYLT verch CYNAN, Queen of Wales, b/abt. 770 in Caer Seiont, Carnarvonshire, Wales, married Merfyn "Frych" ap Gwriad, Prince of Dehubarth and King of Manaw, son of Gwriad Elidir and Nesta Cadell, Queen of Powys. Merfyn "Frych" was b/abt. 764, died 844 in battle of Cyfeiliog, Ketell, Wales.

34. RHODRI "MAWR" (The Great) ap MERFYN, King of all Wales, born 788 at Caer Seiont, Carnarvonshire, Wales, died 877 in Anglesey, Wales. He inherited North Wales from his father, Powys from his mother, and South Wales from his wife, Angharad verch Meurig, Queen of South Wales, daughter of Meurig Dyfnwallon. At the time of his death the three kingdoms were divided among his three sons, as follows:

    35i.   Anarawd, 857-916, was heir to North Wales;

    35ii.   Mervyn, 859-900, was heir to Powys, and his descendant line follows, below.

    35iii. Cadell, 861-910. was heir to South Wales. His descendant line follows that genealogcal line of Mervyn's.

Note: According to legend, the first Dinefwr Castle was built by Rhodri Mawr—King of Wales, in the 9th century. It is unavoidable that attention should focus on those Welsh rulers who extended their power over much of Wales in the centuries prior to the Norman conquest. They foreshadowed the attempts by the princes of Gwynedd in the 13th century to create a unified Welsh state, and they matched contemporary developments in England, and similar, but later, developments in Scotland. So, Rhodri Mawr (844-78) is presented as one who set a pattern for the future. He either ruled or, by his personal qualities, dominated much of Wales.

Chroniclers of his generation hailed Rhodri ap Merfyn as Rhodri Mawr (Rhodri the Great), a distinction bestowed upon two other rulers in the same century—Charles the Great (Charlemagne, died 814) and Alfred the Great (died 899). The three tributes are of a similar nature—recognition of the achievements of men who contributed significantly to the growth of statehood among the nations of the Welsh, the Franks and the English. Unfortunately, the entire evidence relating to the life of Rhodri consists of a few sentences; yet he must have made a deep impression upon the Welsh, for in later centuries being of the line of Rhodri was a primary qualification for their rulers. Until his death, Rhodri was acknowledged as ruler of more than half of Wales, and that as much by diplomacy as by conquest.

Rhodri's fame sprang from his success as a warrior. That success was noted by The Ulster Chronicle and by Sedulius Scottus, an Irish scholar at the court of the Emperor Charles the Bald at Liege. It was his victory over the Vikings in 856 which brought him international acclaim. Wales was less richly provided with fertile land and with the navigable rivers that attracted the Vikings, and the Welsh kings had considerable success in resisting them. Anglesey bore the brunt of the attacks, and it was there in 856 that Rhodri won his great victory over Horn, the leader of the Danes, much to the delight of the Irish and the Franks.

It was not only from the west that the kingdom of Rhodri was threatened. By becoming the ruler of Powys, his mother's land, he inherited the old struggle with the kingdom of Mercia. Although Offa's Dyke had been constructed in order to define the territories of the Welsh and the English, this did not prevent the successors of Offa from attacking Wales. Rhodri was killed in battle against the English in 878.

RHODRI MAWR AND ANGHARAD Verch MEURIG
THREADS FROM THEIR SON, MERVYN

35ii. MERVYN ap RHODRI, King of Powys, born 859, died 900.
36ii. LLEWELYN ap MERVYN, King of Powys.

37ii. ANKARET verch LLEWELYN, Queen of Powys, died 988; married Owen, Prince of Powys, her 2nd cousin (Note: Owen, Prince of Powys, is that same person listed in Penardim).

38ii. MAREDYDD ap OWEN, Prince of Powys, died in 999, married Asritha.

39ii. ANGHARAD verch MAREDYDD, Queen of Powys, married Llewelyn.

RHODRI MAWR AND ANGHARAD Verch MEURIG
THREADS FROM THEIR SON, CADELL

35iii. CADELL ap RHODRI MAWR, born/abt. 861 at Dynevor Castle, Llandyfeisant, Carmarthershire, Wales, died 907 in South Wales, married Rheingar (lnu), born/abt. 865 in Carmarthenshire, Wales. He seized sole power of South Wales by killing his brothers in battle.

36iii. HYWEL DHA (THE GOOD) ap CADELL, born/abt. 887 in Dynevor Castle, Llandyfeisant, Carmarthershire, Wales, died 950 in South Wales. He married Elena verch Llywarch, born/abt. 893 in Dyfed, Wales, daughter of Llywarch ap Hymeid. Hywel Dha was known as "King of the Welsh," ruling over South Wales, Powys, and later North Wales as under king to the Saxon monarchs. Considered a good ruler, he formulated new laws for his country. Note: Hywel Dha and Elena are those persons listed at Generation No. 39, as descendants of Penardim. They were the parents of four sons and one daughter, including: i. Owain ap Howel, born/abt. 913, Dynevor, Llandyfeisant, Carmarthenshire, Wales; died 987. ii. Angharad verch Howell, b. Abt. 920, Dynevor, Llandyfeisant, Carmarthenshire, Wales; married Tudur "Trefor" ap Ynyr, born Abt. 908 in Denbighshire, Wales.

37iii. OWAIN ap HOWEL, born/abt. 913 in Dynevor, Llandyfeisant, Carmarthenshire, Wales, died 987 in South Wales; married Anghared verch Llewelyn, born/abt. 918 in Llandeilo, Carmarthenshire, Wales, died 988, daughter of Llwelyn ap Merfyn.

(Note: Merfyn was the other son of Rhodi "Mawr" and a brother of Cadell and Anarawd at Generation #86). Owain ap Howel and three brothers successfully ruled South Wales jointly, but lost North Wales (Gwynned). After his brothers were killed in fierce battles, Owain became sole prince of South Wales. The children of Owain ap Howel and Anghared verch Llewelyn were: i. Einion ap Owain, b. Abt. 933, Dynevor, Llandyfeisant, Carmarthenshire, Wales; d. 984, Gwent, Monmouthshire, England. ii. Maredydd ap Owain, b. Abt. 938, Dynevor Castle, Llandyfeisant, Carmarthenshire, Wales; d. 999.

38iii. EINON ap OWAIN, born/abt. 913 at Dynevor, Llandyfeisant, Carmarthenshire, Wales, and died 983 in Gwent, Monmouthshire, England. He married Nesta (lnu), born Abt. 934 in Devonshire, England. The eldest son of Owain ap Howel Dda, was, as a young man held in high promise and given command of his father's troops, but was cruelly slain in 983. The Children of Einion Owain and Nesta (lnu) were: i. Cadell ap Einion, born/ abt. 953, Dynevor Castle, Llandyfeisant, Carmarthen- shire, Wales; d. 993, slain in battle. ii. Gronwy ap Einion, born/abt. 959, Dynevor, Llandyfeisant, Carmarthenshire, Wales. He married Ethelfleda verch Edwin, born/abt. 963 in Dynevor, Llandyfeisant, Carmathenshire, Wales.

39iii. CADELL ap EINION, born/abt. 953 in Dynevor Castle, Llandyfeisant, Carmarthen- shire, Wales, and died 993 when he was, with his brother, slain in battle. He married Elinor verch Gwerystan, born/abt. 1007 in Powys, Wales. There only son was: i. Tewdwr "Mawr" ap Cadell, born/abt. 977, Dynevor Castle, Llandyfeisant, Carmarthenshire, Wales.

40iii. TWEDWR "MAWR" ap CADELL, born/abt. 977 in Dynevor Castle, Llandyfeisant, Carmarthenshire, Wales. Having inherited South Wales when his father and uncle was slain in 993, he fled to Brittany to escape the violence of a kinsman, but was there slain in 997. The name of his wife is unknown, but they had one son. i. Rhys ap Twedwr "Mawr", born 997in Brittany, France; died 1093 in Brecon, Breconshire, Wales.

41iii. RHYS "MAWR" ap TWEDWR, was born Abt. 997 in South Wales, and died 1093 in South Wales. He was very young when his

father was slain, and was raised in Brittany. At the age of 80 he returned to successfully stake his claim of sovereignty of South Wales. Records show he paid an annual tribute to William the Conqueror for his land. He was slain in battle in 1093, at the age of 96. He married Gwiadus verch Rhiwallon, born/abt 1041 in Powys, Wales, daughter of Rhiwallon ap Cynfyn. Rhys "Mawr" ap Twedwr and Gwiadus verch Rhiwallon had a son:
i. Gruffudd ap Rhys, born1081, Dynevor Castle, Llandyfeisant, Carmarthen- shire,Wales; d. 1136.

42iii. GRUFFYDD ap RHYS, born 1081 at Dynevor Castle, Llandyfeisant, Carmarthen- shire, Wales, died 1137. The mother of Gruffydd ap Rhys was the last of several wives and he was quite young when his father died. As the eldest surviving son, however, he succeeded to the title, Prince of South Wales. He led an active life sacking and burning. He joined the rebellion against he English and was taken captive, but escaped. He married 1st, Gwellian verch Gruffydd, born/abt. 1090 in Caernarvonshire, Wales, died 1136 (beheaded). She was the daughter of Gruffydd ap Cynan, ruler of Gwynned (North Wales), and the grandfather of Madog, who may have landed in Mobile Bay in 1170. When Gruffydd ap Rhys was taken prisoner by the Brithis, Gwenllian led her husband's troops into battle during her husband's absence in 1136, was defeated, captured, and beheaded. By bloody conquests, however, Gruffydd ap Rhys regained most of his ancestors ancient possessions. Gwellian verch Gruffydd, 1st wife of Gruffydd ap Rhys, was descend-ed from Anarawd, older brother of Cadell ap Rhodri "Mawr," Generation #35i, above, as follows:

Generation #35i, Anarawd ap Rhodri Mawr, born/abt. 857, died 916.
Generation #36i, Idwal "Foel" ap Anarawd, born Abt. 883 in Aberffro, Malltaeth, Anglesey, Wales, and died 942; married Mereddon verch Cadwr, born/abt. 887 in Gwynedd, Wales.
Generation #37i, Meurig ap Idwal, born/abt. 917, Aberffro, Malltaeth, Anglesey, Wales, died 986; wife's name unknown but she was born/abt. 921 n Aberffro, Malltaeth, Anglesey, Wales.

Generation #38i, Idwal ap Meurig, born Abt. 945 in Aberffro, Malltaeth, Anglesey, Wales, died 996 in Battle of Penmynydd, Dindaethwy, Anglesey, Wales. Name of his wife is unknown but she was born/abt. 949 at Aberffraw Castle, Caernavon, Wales.

Generation #39i, Iago ap Idwal, born/abt. 974 in Aberffro, Malltaeth, Anglesey, Wales, died 1039. He married Afandreg verch Gwair Pill, born/abt. 974 in Aberffro, Malltaeth, Anglesey, Wales.

Generation #40i, Cynan ap Iago, born/abt.1014 in Aberffro, Malltaeth, Anglesey, Wales; married Rhanullt O'Olaf, born/abt 1031 in Dublin, Ireland.

Generation #41i, Gruffydd ap Cynan, born 1055 in Caernarvohshire, Wales, died 1137, Caernarvohshire, Wales; married/abt.1082, Angharad verch Owain, born/abt 1065, Tegeingl, Flintshire, Wales, died 1162, daughter of Owain ap Edwin and Morwyl verch Ednywain.

Generation #42i. Gwellian verch Gruffydd ap Cynan, was the 1st wife of Gruffydd ap Rhys, Generation #42, above. Gruffydd ap Rhys was murdered in 1137 by his second wife. The son of Gruffydd ap Rhys and his first wife, Gwellian verch Gruffydd ap Cynan, was Ryes "Fychan" ap Gruffydd, born/abt. 1127, d. 1197.

---

43. RHYS "FYCHAN" ap GRUFFYDD, b. Abt. 1127, died 1197, at Elfaeluwchmynydd, Radnorshire, Wales, died 1197; succeeded his father as Prince of South Wales in 1137. Later, After leading a rebellion against the Crown and losing, he was imprisoned but later released after giving homage to King Henry. He was then made a prisoner by his sons, but later subdued them. Incurring the wrath of a Bishop, he was excommunicated but the ban was later lifted and hewas buried in 1197 in St. David's Cathedral Church, near Dynevor, Wales. While the name of his wife is unknown, they were the parents of Rhys "Gryg" ap Rhys, born/abt. 1167 in Radnorshire, Wales, died/abt. 1233.

44. RHYS "GRYG" ap RHYS, born/abt 1167 in Radnorshire, Wales, died/abt 1233; married Gwerfyl verch Meagwn, born Abt. 1191 in Maelienydd, Radnorshire, Wales. They had several children,

including: i. Madog ap Rhys, born/abt. 1225 at Radnorshire, Wales, died/aft. 1292.

Note: Rhys "Gryg" was the 3rd son of Rhys "Fychan" ap Gruffydd, and succeeded to a large portion of his father's estate. When Rhys Gryg's eldest brother, who had succeeded to Prince of Wales, retired to assume the religious habit, a struggle was waged over succession, with Madog ap Rhys, Rhys

Greg's eldest son by his first wife, gaining the title. Rhys Gryg died of wounds in 1233. Following the death of his 1st wife, Rhys "Grgy" had married 2nd to Joanne de Clare, born/abt. 1185, daughter of Richard de Clare, 6th Earl of Clare, and his wife Amice de Beaumount, Countess of Gloucester. Their son was: ii. Rhys "Miechyll" ap Rhys, aka Rhys Vychan, or Junior, died in 1244, and was buried in Abbey of Tally Llychau.

45. MADOG ap RHYS, born/abt. 1225 at Radnorshire, Wales, died/aft. 1292; married Tanglwyst verch Gronwy, born/abt. 1230 in Gwrinydd, Glamorgan, Wales. They were the parents of: i. Trahaearn "Gooh" ap Madog, born/abt. 1250 at Llyn, Caernarvonshire, Wales; died/aft. 1273, in the Tower of London, London, England.

46. TRAHAEARN "GOOH" ap MADOG, born/abt. 1250 in Llyn, Caernarvonshire, Wales, died 1325 in the Tower of London, London, Middlesex, England. The son of Madog Goch, he held considerable land when he died. He married Gwerful verch Madog, born/abt. 1257 in Maelienydd, Radnorshire, Wales. Their son was: i. Dafydd"Goch" ap Trahaearn, born/abt. 1275, at Penllech, Cymydmaen, Caernar- vonshire, Wales, died/aft. 1324 Bardsey Isle, Aberdaron, Caernarvonshire,

47. DAFYDD"GOCH"apTRAHAEARN, born/abt. 1275, Penllech, Cymydmaen, Caermar- vonshire, Wales, died/aft. 1324 Bardsey Isle, Aberdaron, Caernarvonshire, Wales. He married Mawd (Maud) verch Dafydd, born/abt. 1279 in Rhuddlan, Flintshire, Wales, daughter of Dafydd ap Cynwrig and Annes Gwyn. (Note: Mawd verch Dafydd's name is sometimes anglcized to read

"Maud ap Lloyd, daughter of David Lloyd"). She was descended from Owen Gwynned, Prince of Gwynned, and was also the great- granddaughter of England's King John. Child of Dafydd "Goch" ap Trahaearn and Mawd Verch Dafydd was: i. Ieuan "Goch" ap Dafydd, born/abt. 1310.

48. IEUAN "GOCH" ap DAFYDD, born/abt. 1310, Penllech, Cymydmaen, Caernarvon- shire, Wales. (Ieuan was early Welsh spelling for Evan). The 2nd son of Dafydd "Goch" ap Trahaearn, he married Eva verch Einion ap Cynvelyn. Their son was: i. Madog ap Ieuan "Goch".

49. MADOG ap IEUAN "GOCH," the eldest son, he was born Abt. 1340 in Penllech, Cymydmaen, Caernarvonshire, Wales. He married Alice verch Ieuan, born/abt. 1355 in Cegidfa, Ystradmarchell, Montgomeryshire, Wales, daughter of Ieuan ap Madog and Gwenhwyfar verch Gruffydd. They were the parents of: i. Delcws "Ddu" ap Madog, born/abt. 1375, Penllech, Cymydmaen, Caernarvonshire, Wales.

50. ELCWS "DDU" ap MADOG, born/abt. 1375, Penllech, Cymydmaen, Caernarvon- shire, Wales. In 1398, he served as a Captain under Henry, Duke of Lancaster, against Lord Mowbray. When Henry was banished by King Richard for ten years and Mowbray for life, Delcws "Ddu" was thereafter indicted as a felon and traitor, and had his lands forfeited. He married Gwen verch Ieuan, born/abt. 1379 in Arllech- wedd Isaf, Caenarvio-shire, Wales. They were the parents of: i. Einon ap Deicws, born/abt. 1415, Yspytty Evan, Is Aled, Denbighshire, Wales.

51. EINION ap DEICWS, born/abt. 1415, Yspytty Evan, Is Aled, Denbighshire, Wales. He was the youngest son of Deicws Ddu ap Madog he married Morfudd verch Mathew, born/abt. 1419 in Merionethshire, Wales. They were the parents of: i. Hywel (Hwita) ap Einion, born/abt. 1456, Yspytty Eva, Is Aled, Denbighshire, Wales, died 1543.

52. HOWEL (HWITA) ap EINION, was born/abt.1456 in Yspytty Evan, Is Aled, Denbigh- shire, Wales, and died 1543. The eldest son of Einion ap Dwikws, he served as an archer under his cousin in 1485. He married Mali "Llwyd" verch Llewelyn, born/abt.

1460 in Lal, Denbighshire, Wales, daughter of Llewlyn Ieuan and Dyddgu verch Einion. They were the parents of: i. Gruffydd ap Howel, born/aby. 1488, Yspytty Evan, Is Aled, Denbighshire, Wales.

53. GRUFFYDD ap HOWEL (HWITA), b. Abt. 1488, Yspytty Evan, Is Aled, Denbighshire, Wales, he lived and died in the parish of Yspytty Evan, Denbighshire, Wales. He married Gwenllian ap Einion, born/abt. 1492 in Llansannan, Denbighshire, Wales, daughter of Einion Ieuan and Gwenhyf verch Gronwy. They were the parents of: i. Lewis ap Gruffydd, born 1525, Yspytty Evan, Denbighshire, Wales.

54. LEWIS ap GRUFFYDD, born 1525, Yspytty Evan, Denbighshire, Wales; died1600 in Yshute, Yspytty Evan, Denbighshire, Wales. Note: He was the 3rd son of Gruffydd ap Howell and his ancestors are listed in "Welsh Founders of Pennsylvania," authored by Howard M. Jenkins, Chapter XIII, and summarized in his descent from Mervyn Vryen (King of Man, killed in battle with the King of Mercia in A.D. 843), who married Essylt, daughter and sole heiress of the King of Wales. Lewis ap Gruffydd (anglicized To Griffith) married Ellen ap Edward, born/ abt. 1520 in Llenwddyn, Montgomery- shire, Wales, daughter of Edward Evan and his wife Catherine.They were the parents of: i. Robert ap Lewis, born 1555, Yspytty Evan, Denbighshire, Wales, died 1647,Yspytty Evan, Denbighshire, Wales.

55. ROBERT ap LEWIS, b. 1555, Yspytty Evan, Denbighshire, Wales; d. 1637, Yspytty Evan, Denbighshire, Wales. He married Gwerfyl ap Llewelyn, born/abt. 1550, Llarirwst, Denbighshire, Wales, daughter of Llewelyn ap David. Their son was: i. Evan ap Robert Lewis, b/abt. 1584, Yspytty Evan, Denbighshire, Wales. 56. EVAN ap ROBERT LEWIS, aka Llwyd (Lloyd), was the 4th son of Robert Lewis. He was born abt. 1584 at Yspytty Evan, Denbighshire, later moving from Rhiwlas to Vron Goch, Merionethshire, Wales, where he spent the remainder of his life. Described as an honest, sober man, he married Uron Goch (aka Jane) born/abt. 1585, died abt. 1662, daughter of Cadwaladr ap Maredydd. The five sons of Evan ap Robert Lewis took for themselves the surname of Evan. One of those five

sons was: i. Rev. Evan Lloyd Evan, born/abt. 1634, Llanfor, Vron Goch, Merionethshire, Wales.

57. REV. EVAN LLOYD EVAN, born/abt. 1634, Llanfor, Vron Goch, Merionethshire, Wales, died April 25, 1690, Llanfor Church, near Vron Goch, Caernarvonshire, Wales. Vron Goch, Caernarvonshire, Wales. Evan Lloyd Evan, (aka Evan ap Evan and Evan Evans), was the 5th son of Evan ap Robert Lewis. An Episcopal minister, he died and was buried 25 April 1690 at Llanfor Church, near Vron Goch, Caernarvonshire, Wales. By his 2nd wife, whose name is unknown, he had four sons and a daughter, Namely: Thomas, Robert, Owen, Cadwalader, and Sarah. All five children immigrated in 1698 to Gwynned, Pennsylvania, along with the husband of Sarah, Robert Pugh. Of these:

58. SARAH ap EVAN, born abt. 1665 in Llanfor, Vron Goch, Merionethshire, Wales, and died in Gwynned, Pennsylvania. She married abt. 1695 to Robert ap Hugh Pugh, in Llandderfel Parsh, Merionethshire, Wales. He was born 1670 in Bala, Merioneth- shire, Wales, and died in Gwynned, Pennsylvania. They were the parents of:

59. EVAN PUGH. He immigrated to Pennsylvania with his parents, and married Mary (lnu). They later moved to Virginia, and were the parents of a son, Jesse Pugh.

60. JESSE PUGH. The records are not clear about Jesse Pugh, and it was long believed he was the son of Robert and Sarah (Evans) Pugh. But it has been established they were his grandparents; Jesse being instead the son of Evan Pugh. The name of his wife is not known, but he was the father of Robert Pugh, who was a pioneer to the Cacapon Valley in Hampshire County, Virginia (now West Virginia).

61. ROBERT PUGH, SR., born 7 Oct1730 in Pennsylvania, died between 1801—1808 in Cacapon Valley, Hampshire Co., Virginia (now West Virginia). He married on 8 Jan 1756 to Mary Edwards, born between1730-1740, died/aft.1824 at Cacapon Valley, Hampshire Co., Va. (now West Virginia), the daughter of Joseph Edwards, Jr., born/abt. 1796, Concord Twp., Chester co., Pa., died/aft. 10 Apr 1781 at Cacapon Valley, Hampshire

co., Va. (now WV), who married bef. 1741 in Frederick co., Va., to Sarah Nalley, born/aft. 1699 in Frederick co., Va., and died at Cacapon Valley Hampshire co., Va. (now WV). Note: Joseph Edwards, Jr., was the builder of Fort Edwards, constructed on his 400 acre farm in the Cacapon Valley, encompassing the present*day town of Capon Bridge, Hampshire County, West Virginia. Robert Pugh and Mary Edwards were the parents of fourteen children, including Mary Pugh.

62. MARY PUGH, born 29 Jan 1762 at Cacapon Valley, Hampshire Co., Va., (now West Virginia); died 1 Feb1849 at Beverly, Randolph Co., Va. (now West Virginia), married on 7 Jan 1779 in Hampshire co., Va. (now West Virginia) to John Chenoweth, born 15 Nov 1755 in Frederick co., Virginia, died 16 Jan 1831 at Beverly, Randolph co., Va. (now West Virginia, son of William Chenoweth and Ruth Calvert. Their esdest child was Robert Chenoweth.

63. ROBERT CHENOWETH, born 19 Apr 1782, Randolph Co., Va. (now West Virginia); died 21 May1862 at Nicut, Calhoun Co., Va. (now West Virginia); married 1st on 23 Aug 1802, at at Beverly, Randolph Co., Va. (WV), to Rachel Stalnaker. They had 3 daughters. After the death of his 1st wife, Robert Chenoweth married, 2nd, on 11 Apr 1811, Pendleton co., Va. (WV), Edith Skidmore, born 15 Sep 1788 at Ruddle, Pendleton co., Va. (WV), died 17 Nov 1857, Nicut, Calhoun Co.,Va. (WV). She was The daughter of John Skidmore and Mary Magdalena Hinkle. Robert and Edith Skidmore Chenoweth were the parents of 10 children, including:

64. SUSANNAH CHENOWETH, born 29 Apr 1812, Beverly, Randolph co., Va. (now West Virginia), died 20 Apr 1862 at Reedy, Roane co., West Virginia. She married on 19 Nov 1830 at Beverly, Randolph Co., Va. (WV) to John Stalnaker, born 6 Nov 1804, Beverly, Randolph Co., Va. *WV), died 30 Mar 1862, Reedy, Roane Co., WV. son of George Washington Stalnaker and Susannah Hart, daughter of Edward Hart and Nancy Ann Stout.

65. MARTHA ANN STALNAKER, born 1 Feb 1834, at Beverly, Randolph Co., Va. (now WV), died 15 Sep 1870 on Cox`s Fork,

Harper Dist., Roane Co., West Virginia. She married on 19 June 1851 in Wirt Co., Va. (now WV) to Robert Hopkins, born 23 Dec 1822, Pendleton Co., Va (now WV), died 10 Feb 1894, at Round Knob, Roane Co., WV, son of Lawrence Braddock Hopkins and Mary "Polly" Jordan. They were the parents of 4 daughters and 4 sons, including:

66.   ALBERT JENNINGS FLOYD3 HOPKINS, born 17 Jul 1862 on Flat Fork, Harper Dist., Roane Co., WV, died 03 Mar 1938 at Wanego, Geary Dist., Roane Co., WV. He married , 30 Dec 1885 at Wanego, Geary Dist., Roane Co., WV, to Martha Marcina Gandee, born 23 Nov 1866 at Gandeeville, Roane Co., WV, died 13 Nov 1946 at Wanego (now Newton), Roane Co., WV, daughter of Frederick Gandee and Caroline Canterbury. The only son of Floyd Hopkins and Martha Gandee was:

67.   ROBERT FREDRICK HOPKINS, born 09 Sep 1890 in Wanego (Newton P.O.), Geary Dist., Roane Co., WV, died 29 May 1953 in Charleston, Kanawha Co., WV. He married 17 Jul 1911 at Bloomington, Roane Co., WV, to Nora Catherine Cook, born 28 Oct 1892 at Bloomington (Amma P.O.), Geary Dist., Roane Co., WV, died 05 Jan 1969 in Charleston, Kanawha Co., WV, daughter of Aaron Cook and Mary D.M. Drake. Their eldest child was:

68.   THELMA EVELYN HOPKINS, born 16 Aug 1912 at Bloomington (Amma P.O.), Geary Dist., Roane Co., WV; died 17 Oct 1979 in Orrville, Wayne Co., Ohio. She married on 20 Apr 1930 at Clendenin, Kanawha Co., WV, (license issued: Roane Co.), to Gerald Leo Cruikshank, Sr., born 08 Mar 1908 in Middle Creek, Clay Co., WV, died 17 Aug 1971 in the VA Hospital, Huntington, Wayne Co., WV, son of Oscar Evert Cruikshank and Lois Morton. Gerald L. Cruikshank, Sr and Thelma Evelyn Hopkins were the parents of 3 daughters and 3 sons.

Note: The above persons at Generation #68, are the same as those persons listed in Generation #75 in the line of descendants shown from Parnardim, daughter of Anna and Joseph of Arimathea.

ABOUT THE AUTHOR OF THIS BOOK

Robert Cruikshank was born at Newton, West Virginia, and spent fourteen years in the U.S. Air Force prior to becoming an ordained minister in the United Methodist Church. He has served churches in the Alabama-West Florida and the West Virginia Annual Conferences. He has received degrees from Troy and Emory Universities.

In 1989, he briefly served as an exchange pastor at Central Church, in Torquay, Devonshire, England. It was during a tour arranged by that church's parishioners to Glastonbury Abbey that he encountered the story of Joseph of Arimathea, Saint Mary's Chapel, and The Holy Thorn.

Married for 62 years to his high school sweetheart, the former Sharon Lynn Griffin, they live in a little patch of woods just south of Greenville, Alabama. They are the parents of 3 children, 5 grandchildren, and 10 great-grandchildren who richly bless their golden days.

He retired in 1994 from appointive ministry in the West Virginia Annual Conference, however, he continues to serve as Associate Pastor at First United Methodist Church, Greenville, Alabama.